Zachariah Atwell Mudge

The Luck of Alden Farm

With a sketch of the history of Crane's Corner

Zachariah Atwell Mudge

The Luck of Alden Farm
With a sketch of the history of Crane's Corner

ISBN/EAN: 9783337011482

Printed in Europe, USA, Canada, Australia, Japan

Cover: Foto ©ninafisch / pixelio.de

More available books at **www.hansebooks.com**

THE

LUCK OF ALDEN FARM:

WITH

A SKETCH OF THE HISTORY OF CRANE'S CORNER,

WHERE "LUCK" WAS SLOWLY LEARNED.

THE WHOLE INTENDED AS A SAFE GUIDE OF ALL YOUNG
PEOPLE TO "GOOD LUCK."

BY

REV. Z. A. MUDGE,
AUTHOR OF "SHELL COVE," ETC.

Boston:
Published by D. Lothrop & Co.
Dover, N. H.: G. T. Day & Co.
1873.

Entered, according to Act of Congress, in the year 1873,
By D. LOTHROP & CO.,
In the Office of the Librarian of Congress, at Washington.

CONTENTS.

CHAPTER I.
A HINT, ... 5
CHAPTER II.
SUNSHINE, ... 17
CHAPTER III.
SHADOWS, ... 35
CHAPTER IV.
THE CHILDRENS' MEETING, ... 50
CHAPTER V.
THE RAISING, ... 63
CHAPTER VI.
MORE LUCK AT ALDEN FARM, ... 76
CHAPTER VII.
THE HUSKING, ... 95
CHAPTER VIII.
AFTER THE HUSKING, ... 115
CHAPTER IX.
THE NEW SCHOOLMASTER, ... 136
CHAPTER X.
A BREEZE AT CRONE'S CORNER, ... 152
CHAPTER XI.
THE WINTER SCHOOL, ... 175
CHAPTER XII.
THE EXAMINATION, ... 200

CONTENTS.

CHAPTER XIII.
Patty Vose, ... 219

CHAPTER XIV.
Studying by Rule, ... 239

CHAPTER XV.
"Mose Pond," 255

CHAPTER XVI.
A New Life, ... 277

CHAPTER XVII.
Burdened Hearts, ... 297

CHAPTER XVIII.
The Comforter, ... 318

CHAPTER XIX.
The Deceivers and the Deceived, ... 330

CHAPTER XX.
Lonely and Comfortless, ... 349

CHAPTER XXI.
The Angel Helper, ... 368

CHAPTER XXII.
The Jubilee, ... 380

THE LUCK OF ALDEN FARM.

CHAPTER I.

A HINT.

THE homestead of Alden Farm, as a whole, is, at the time of our story, a good specimen of the New England homesteads of "the olden time." The old chimney is there, in the center of the house, and contains bricks enough for all the chimneys of three, first class, modern farm houses. But the old fireplace, its settle, huge crane, large, winter back-logs, around whose great fire the children could scarcely keep comfortably warm, and up whose immense flue the heat rushed, into the thin, cold atmosphere, as if bravely seeking to warm "all out doors,"—this old fire-place, we say, is not there.

The proprietor—we mean plain John Alden, the farmer and owner of the house and its farm—does not retain old things because they are old, nor reject proposed changes because they are new. He was in the prime of life when cooking-stoves were proposed as a substitute for the old fire-place. John, when in town with a load of his best oak wood, which had begun to bring "a good price"—say three dollars and a half a cord, stepped into a stove dealer's to look at "the new notion." The man of stoves, with a sharp eye to trade, opened its doors to exhibit its fire-range, oven and drafts, paraded its shining furniture, with a proud air, as much as to say, "Mister, see that!" and talked the while in a manner which meant trade.

John Alden whistled, thrust his hands into his pockets, examined the article closely, made little talk with the man, and finally stood some minutes in musing silence.

"What's the price of that arrangement?" said John, breaking the silence.

"Only thirty-six dollars!" said the stove man, blandly.

"I'll talk with Patience about it," said John, turning resolutely away.

John mounted the seat of his heavy ox-wagon, and rode off whistling, while the disappointed man of trade walked back to his bench, muttering, "The simpleton don't know his mind, but must ask his old woman at home! Such old fellows would not pay thirty-six dollars for all the improvements in Christendom!"

"I'll take that article," said John Alden, just three weeks from this time, as he walked into the stove dealer's place of business, at the same time drawing a purse of silver dollars from his pocket.

John and his wife, Patience, had talked

the matter over beside their huge fire-place. They carefully noted the increasing value of wood; they called to mind the cold drafts from the opened doors, during the winter, and the hot drafts which went roaring up the chimney; John explained what he deemed the conveniences of the new invention — its saving of labor and fuel; and, finally, the great outlay of thirty-six hard dollars, earned by hard toil, was balanced, with careful reckoning, against these advantages. When the decision was once made, John and Patience went quietly at work, as assured that their decision was right, as if it had been considered by a jury of the fathers of the town, and they had rendered their verdict in due form.

John and Patience Alden were not self-conceited people, but they did have "a mind of their own," as even the stove-man now believed, and a self-reliance which was remarkably fruitful of good luck.

The mason was called to wall up, with brick and mortar, the ancestral fire-place. The man with the trowel worked away, but grumbled as he worked, "It is none of my business, Patience Alden, and I am not a man to be meddling with other people's affairs. But it does seem to me that John is real foolish. I heard my mother tell how his good old grandparents sat before this very fire-place, resting and chatting, and then getting out the great family Bible, just as people *used* to do, when new fangled things wan't so much thought of. And then, Patience, haven't I seen, since your day in this house, John's own dear father and mother, sitting right here, in this place which I'm shutting up never to be seen again, drinking their cider of a cold winter evening, and a thanking God for their own home and hearth? Dear me, what would they say! Well, they have gone where they won't be troubled with these times of pride and nonsense."

Patience dropped a tear at the allusion to the greatly beloved parents, which the bricklayer mistook for a tear of regret at John's foolish purchase; so he added with increased earnestness, "Patience Alden, I never thought *you* were to blame for this foolish business. It don't seem like John neither. He's been real lucky, and got ahead smartly. But it don't signify, he's missed it this time!"

Patience wiped the tears from her face, at this reflection upon her husband, and turned to the meddler, with a quiet but resolute countenance, as she exclaimed, "John and I are perfectly agreed concerning this improvement!"

The man subsided into a becoming silence during the rest of his stay in the house.

John Alden's neighbor, Mr. Crone, and his wife, Jerusha Crone, and all the little Crones, let fly their sharp arrows, that is, their bitter words, at John and his wife, for their late extravagance.

"I can't afford to spend thirty-six hard-earned dollars to gratify my wife's foolish notion for a new thing."

"You may thank your good fortune," said Mrs. Crone, smartly, "that your wife has no foolish notion after new things."

"I know it, woman," said Mr. Crone, in a conciliatory manner. "We always get along nicely in the good old paths. I told the parish committee, when they came round to make up the salary of the parson, that I should pay only the two cords of wood, which I have always paid, and which my father and grandfather paid. 'It was enough,' said I, 'for their minister, and it's enough for mine.' But, Jerusha, I believe they would have teased another cord from me, had you not given them a piece of your mind about the extravagance of the times."

All the little Crones caught the spirit of their parents. Ezekiel, or "Zeke," as they called him, said, petulantly, "The Alden boys always did feel big. Now they will be grander than ever!" And Zake gave his "chip hat" a toss into the air, and a kick when it came down, transferring to his innocent hat the ill will he felt to the lucky children of Alden Farm.

Neighbor Goodnow thought that John and Patience knew what they were about. "For my part," he said, "I would not risk the throwing away of thirty-six hard-earned dollars, but I shan't matter it, if John's experiment proves saving. It's a blessing to have a man like John among folks, who is willing to take all the risk of new things."

Goodnow represented a class of John's neighbors, who were sure to reap a benefit from his spirit of enterprise. If his plans succeeded, they adopted them; if they failed, they were wiser in their own eyes than before, exclaiming complacently, "We told you so, John! That was a silly notion of yours!"

John Alden and his wife were fully informed by the gossipers concerning the talk of their neighbors. But they were neither angry nor disturbed. He sometimes laughed heartily at their expense. He could generally afford to do this, for his plans were adopted with caution, and patient thinking, and then carried out with decision. So he laughed when his neighbors grumbled, and felt the better for it, especially as his healthful laughing did them no hurt.

John's stove was set up, and in due time the winter came. In the time of which we speak, the winter, like the early Puritan society, was a positive "institution." The fall did not shade into the winter, and the winter into the spring, so that one was at loss to tell whether the winter had been absorbed by these two seasons, or whether there had been no season in particular, as in these degenerate times. The cold came on, like a genuine article as it was, direct from the Arctic regions. The snow was a home product, and in quality and quantity did credit to the sturdy old character of the New England climate.

The great kitchen of Alden Farm smiled "all over its face," as the little Aldens diligently supplied the stove, in a stormy winter evening, with well seasoned, oak wood; it did not smile, as in the days of the huge fire-place, on one side of its face with the rosy hue of summer heat, and on the other scowl with a biting frost. The old kitchen was jubilant with the stove's genial warmth, and so were the kitchen's inmates. The little Aldens, with whom, in a larger growth we are to become acquainted, sat around a table at one end of the room. Their parents sat at the little "snap stand" at the other. The young folks liked this; their pent-up laughter and sly fun were under less restraint than when the family were huddled about the now cast-off back log. The par ents liked it, because, sitting by themselves, they had more quiet, a better chance to indulge in their own line of talk, and, especially because they did not *choose* to see and hear all that their children did. John and Patience did enjoy immensely to see the young folks fairly sparkle and run over at times, with youthful animation. They knew when such outbursts had the right moral tone, and they knew how not to be nervous at their noise, and when not to put their hands on the escaping steam, and so how not to scald themselves; and how not to blow up the children.

John Alden cut the usual generous pile of wood that winter. He did not spend his time loitering in the kitchen, because it was more comfortable than usual. When the Crones saw his wood-pile, larger, as they thought, than ever, they shrugged their shoulders and said, "John don't expect to save any fuel by his new notion, after all!"

But before the summer was ended, he had sold in town enough wood saved by the stove to replace more than half of those thirty-six dollars which so troubled his neighbors.

"It is the luck of Alden Farm folks to have things come out just so!" exclaimed the Crones. "Every wind is fair for them. *We* never did have any luck." But deacon Turner said in his quiet way that he thought that the luck at Alden Farm was nothing more than God's blessing on the exercise of good sense, and the putting forth of a genuine Yankee energy.

CHAPTER II.

SUNSHINE.

It was a bitter cold evening of the winter in which the "new notion" was introduced into the great kitchen of Alden Farm. The snow was drifting in heavy banks about the door-ways and across every pathway. When a gust of wind unusually fierce rattled the sleet against the windows, Carver, the oldest son, pushed the elbow of Miles, who sat by his side absorbed in a book he was reading, and exclaimed, "Hear that Miles, don't it come good! I guess it will be fun to-morrow wading to school through the snow!"

Miles looked up for a moment, remarked dreamily that it did storm splendidly, and dropped his eyes again upon his book.

The youngest child, the baby Winslow, was asleep in the cradle, on the rocker of which Mrs. Alden's foot was resting, while her hands were busily engaged in mending some rather large holes in the stockings of the boys. Her husband sat on the other side of the table, with folded hands, in a musing attitude. His face at last relaxed into a humorous expression, not uncommon in his familiar intercourse with his family, as he bent down and whispered to his wife, "Patience, can you say your lesson in the Catechism?"

Mrs. Alden, a little startled, said with a slight expression of doubt as to the meaning of the question, "I am not a child, John, to be getting a lesson in the Catechism."

John smiled, but answered seriously, "No, Patience, but the minister said last Sunday, that the children would meet on Saturday following the Wednesday-lecture, in the big kitchen of the parsonage, with their Catechisms, and he should know what members neglected the religious instruction of their children. Now, Patience, you know we haven't neglected this duty altogether, but it don't stand to reason that the children will learn from us what we don't know ourselves."

"Do you mean, John," said Patience, laying down her half darned stocking and looking at her husband with a shade of severity upon her usually calm face, "that we ought to go to the parsonage and say our Catechism with the children, to prove to them that we know what it teaches?"

"No, Patience," replied Mr. Alden, with a merry twinkle of his eye. "You need only to recite to *me!*"

"Oh!" replied Mrs. Alden, pleasantly, resuming her work, "if that is all, you can get the Catechism and proceed."

John took down from the book-case one of several carefully preserved copies of the important little book, and commenced a very slow and hesitating questioning of his wife. Patience's face wore a devout expression, but her attention seemed not to be diverted a moment from her work, while she answered every question as readily as though the answers had been the last committed lessons of a girl of sixteen. John, surprised, put the questions more rapidly and with less caution as to being heard by the children. He ran through many sections of the book, and then skipped here and there, picking out questions which involved long and difficult answers. But Patience, nowhere, for a moment tripped.

"Nicely done," said Mr. Alden, laying down the book and pushing back his chair, as if he was about to walk the room as he often did.

"Stop, John," said Patience, the twinkle this time being in her eye; "it don't stand to reason that you can insist upon the children knowing the Catechism, without you can answer its questions yourself. Let me hear *you!*"

John blushed a little, but drew his chair up again to the table and waited for the questions. Patience proceeded very seriously and slowly to put them. The answers for some time, though very deliberately given, were correct. But when his wife began to skip about, and select random questions, John plead a bad memory, and declared he would read nothing but the Bible and Catechism until he could answer every one.

Carver and Miles, at their table, on the other side of the room, were listening to this Catechism recitation. They laughed a little slyly when father stumbled at the answers, and Carver whispered in his brother's ear that mother was "too wide-awake" for father.

"Maybe she catches him now," answered Miles, in an undertone, "but I reckon father will answer all the questions like a book, after about two evenings."

The storm increased at a fearful rate. Mr. Alden lit the lamp in the lantern and went to the barn to see if "all was right." The thought that a barn door might have been accidently left open, or the bedding of some of the animals neglected, urged this special care. Mrs. Alden had more precious subjects of interest on her mind. She took the candle from the old mantle-piece and went up stairs to see if the sleepers in the trundle-bed, Ruth and Rachel, were "warm and comfortable." She tucked them up anew, laid an additional blanket over their feet, paused a moment to look at the cozy nestlers and say, "God bless them," and then to examine carefully everything through the chambers that the cold could injure.

While the parents were absent on these errands of kindness and love, the sons discussed in their way the parental study of the Catechism.

"Mother did answer the questions splendidly," remarked Carver.

"Yes," said Miles, "but father didn't do bad. I reckon though women can always beat the men in answering smart and lively. How the girls do beat us, Carver, at school!"

Carver was taken by surprise at this allusion, and blushed a little, for Squire Treen's daughter had gone above him that day in the class, by answering a question he had missed. He defended himself and his sex by answering more sharply than the occasion required, "They don't understand the lessons though half as well as the boys!"

The return of the parents suppressed the reply of Miles, but not his merry laugh at his brother's expense.

The family of John Alden were astir long before the daylight appeared. Ruth and Rachel had been "lively as crickets," long before a light was brought for them to dress; while Miles had pestered out of his brother a disposition to take another doze, by plying him with all the Catechism questions he could think of. "I'll pay you, Miles, for this," he yawned, "by putting you through the whole book when I get up."

"It won't be fair," retorted Miles, "to put me through any thing but the lesson we are to say to the minister on Saturday afternoon."

"Yes, the *whole* book," persisted his brother. "When I was twelve years old I could answer every question as quick as a hen can pick up a kernel of corn."

Miles received this brag with a chuckle. "If he did it at twelve, he ought to do it at fourteen years old," he mused. "Sometime, when he gets deep into his study, I'll come down upon him, with questions in the Catechism, thick and fast as hail stones. Carver will be up with me though if I don't know every answer in the book; I did almost, once."

"Feeling his spirit stirred by these musings, Miles exclaimed, aloud, "Here's the boy —" he was about to say, "Here's the boy that can conquer it!" but seeing his brother start up with wonder at his earnestness, he stopped suddenly and settled down calmly upon his knees to offer his morning prayer. He then went down stairs, followed soon by his brother, and both immediately engaged cheerfully in assisting their parents; the older one in the barn with the father, and the younger in the kitchen.

At Alden Farm, before there were daughters old enough to be efficient in domestic work, the sons in turn, "helped mother." She often had for them "a tale of other days," which had descended through the household circles, from the early Pioneer settlers, or a song which equally well made cheerful hearts and willing hands. So Carver and Miles often prepared the vegetables for the meals, sat the table, or washed the dishes, with such pleasant beguilement of the time, that they almost reluctantly left the kitchen for the more appropriate boys' work of the barn. There was no degradation felt or thought of. Their mother's presence made honorable the hour, and the work.

On the morning of which we were speaking, Miles, with his eight year old sister, Ruth, did much of the morning work of the kitchen. Rachel, six years old, was full of glee, and the three summers Jeremiah, was ready at every turn, with his childish pranks, while the baby, Winslow, did all the scolding for the family. *He* was hungry, wanted his breakfast, and would have it, whether anybody else was served or not. In vain Jeremiah chided. "Naughty, naughty baby!" he said, solemnly; "don't you know mother is werry busy? Itty boys should wait."

But baby only kicked the sides of the cradle more spitefully, and, if louder screams meant anything, exclaimed, "I won't wait!"

"Itty ki-baby," said Jeremiah, putting his lips as near the enraged animal in the cradle as he dared to.

"You little Sancho," said Ruth, shaking her fist at him.

Baby's mother came to the rescue at last, the family were permitted by his cradle majesty to eat their breakfast and attend to family devotions in peace, and Miles soon after was told by his mother, with one of her sweetest smiles, that he might go.

"You may go, my son," was all that was *said*. But to Miles, when he looked into her loving eyes, it *meant*,—You have done your work well; helped me a great deal; God bless you!

There was nobody to chide Miles for sitting cosily beside the stove with his book. It was his school book which was first studied, and kept in his lap. But he slyly drew out his Catechism once in a while, and gave its pages close attention. He was determined to surprise not only his brother Carver, but his parents, by his ability to answer every question.

Monday evening before the Saturday childrens' meeting at the parsonage, the Alden family were around their evening lamps. It was very early, the twilight still lingering outside. As the breakfast at the farm-house was eaten long before daybreak, the dinner hour came at twelve, or even earlier, and the supper at five, or, not unfrequently, as on this evening, at half past four. The solemn stillness of dream-land pervaded the house at nine, unless the baby Winslow forbade it.

On this occasion, Ruth and Rachel had not yet gone to their trundle-bed. There was little study, but much merriment, with the boys while they were present.

"Look here, Miles!" said Carver, suddenly, as if a bright thought had just occurred to him, "next Saturday is the Catechism day at the parsonage. I must see that you know all your Catechism. Stand up now, hold up your head, and speak so as to be heard."

Miles reached out his hand and seized the Catechism, with which Carver was about to proceed, and said, in a most solemn tone, while he quoted the words of his father, "It don't stand to reason that we should require of others what we don't know ourselves. I will see how well *you* can answer the questions."

Carver was fairly caught, and submitted, in imitation of his father's example, to be examined, and came out of the trial remarkably well, stumbling on a few answers only.

"T-o-l-e-r-a-b-l-y well, my boy," drawled out Miles, in imitation of the old gentleman who taught the district school. "You may sit down and study one hour, and you will know it perfectly."

Carver had good sense and kind feeling

enough to enjoy the pleasantry he had himself commenced, and he sat down to his hour's task, indulging the thought that his turn would come for fun, at the end of the hour, when he would come down on Miles "like night," with questions from the Catechism.

In the meantime, Miles turned to Ruth, and proposed to examine her.

"It don't stand to reason that you should hear me until I hear you," said Ruth, pertly, catching up the Catechism and beginning to ask him the questions. Carver enjoyed this hugely, but Miles answered every question. He won't get along so well when *I* examine him, thought Carver. I'll be thorough.

Ruth went through her assigned lesson promptly, and turned to Rachel, who repeated what she had learned from her mother's lips.

"Now, Jerry," said Rachel, turning to her little brother, "I must hear you!"

"No!" said Jerry, throwing back his shoulders, and putting on a lordly air as he lisped, "'Oo shan't! It don't stand weeson."

The children shouted applause, clapped their hands, and told Jerry to put Rachel through his Primer lesson. But he was content with having shaken his sister off, and ran away to the cradle, where baby Winslow lay, bestowing his sweetest smiles upon all who came near.

"Hurrah!" shouted Ruth, "he is going to examine the baby!"

All the children started at once for the cradle.

"Ask baby who made him!" said Miles, patting Jerry coaxingly on his shoulder.

Jerry put his lips close to Winnie's face and lisped, "Who made 'oo, Winnie? Don't 'oo know? God made 'oo."

"Ask him more!" shouted Rachel, "see how knowing he looks!"

"What did he—" proceeded Rachel, prompting Jerry.

"What did he make 'oo for, Minnie?" said Jerry, reaching still further into the cradle. "Don't 'oo know? He didn't make 'oo to ki and be a naughty baby. He made 'oo to be good."

"That will do, children," said Mrs. Alden, waving the children away with her hand. "That is as much as Winslow's little brain can bear to-night."

Ruth and Rachel were, in a few moments, tucked away in their cozy bed; Winnie, exhausted by his great mental efforts in his first lesson concerning God and his duty to him, followed his equally tired teacher to the blessed sleep-land. Miles answered Carver's thorough questioning so perfectly, that the latter, much to his disappointment, did not find occasion to require him to review the Catechism. Quiet reigned for a while in the great kitchen, except as the old clock in the corner audibly announced the departure of each precious moment as it flitted past.

"Patience!" said John Alden, breaking the silence by addressing his wife in an undertone of great tenderness and solemnity, "what wonderful truths the Catechism does teach. I never felt their importance as I do now. I think I begin to have a better understanding of them."

Mrs. Alden laid down her work and looked at him seriously, but with a joyful expression, while her husband was uttering these words. They were the language of her own heart. "Yes, John," she replied. "I am glad there is so much of Christ in the Catechism; there is so much in the Bible!"

Mr. and Mrs. Alden then dropped into a quiet conversation about these wonderful truths. The more they talked about them the more their hearts glowed with the inward experience of their wonderful power. "Isn't it wonderful!" "How precious!" were frequent exclamations from Mr. Alden, to which his wife would add; "It is just as I read it, John, in the Word of God. It is Christ from the beginning to the end. He *is* a divine Saviour!"

The boys were attracted by this earnest, melting talk. The parents scarcely noticed the fact that they had left their end of the room, and taken seats, as deeply interested listeners.

"Miles!" said Carver, as they retired, "I begin to like the Catechism. I used to think it was as dry as a chip."

"I think I *ought* to love it," said Miles, seriously. "How happy father and mother did get over it! Their talk has helped me to understand many hard questions. I have been afraid the minister would ask me what they meant. Now if he does, I can answer."

The visit to the parsonage was anticipated by the children of Alden Farm with much pleasure.

CHAPTER III.

SHADOWS.

"Now, Mr. Ezekiel Crone, I desire you would listen to me for once," said Mr. Crone's wife, Jerusha. He knew this mode of address meant business, so he stood in the middle of the great kitchen, in his farmer's frock, and hat in hand, and listened. Mrs. Crone took her hands out of the pumpkin she was pressing through a "cullender" for her pies, and turned her resolute face toward her meek looking husband.

"Ezekiel, you heard Parson Curtis say that on Saturday, three weeks, the children of the parish are required to be present at the parsonage to be examined in the Catechism?"

Ezekiel nodded assent. He certainly had heard the notice.

"Well," proceeded Mrs. Crone, "our Zeke and Tom ought and *shall* go."

Mr. Crone was passive under this declaration, but his wife added a spur to his indecision. "It's a *shame*, Ezekiel, that *our* children, members as we are of the church, know nothing about that important little book! Mercy knows it's not *my* fault, for I have scolded enough about it."

Ezekiel gave a slight nod of assent to this, and his wife thus encouraged, continued, "When I was a girl I could repeat the answers to more'n half the questions, right off." After this self-satisfying remark, Mrs. Crone dropped her voice into a softened tone and asked, "Ezekiel, could you ever do as well as that?"

Her husband had an indistinct recollection of having tried once to get a lesson in the Catechism, but he thought it quite unreasonable for any one to expect him to know anything about it now. To this his wife assented, saying, "It don't stand to reason that we should know the Catechism. The parson won't examine us neither. But the boys *shall* learn it."

Ezekiel nodded assent, and his wife turned to her pumpkin pie making. She hustled the small children, Jane and Betsey, a little more roughly than ever, and sharply prompted the boys in their chore business.

"Don't you think, Tom," said Zeke, "that there's a storm brewing?"

Tom turned his eye up to the stars which sparkled with unusual brilliancy in the clear, cold atmosphere, and replied, "No, Zeke, there's not a cloud to be seen."

"I mean in the kitchen," said his brother, smiling softly.

"I hope not," said Tom, "for if it comes, it will be sure to blow my school lesson away. I am most up to the head of my class for once, and I am determined to show the boys that a Crone *can* do something.

Bill Short did vex me awfully this afternoon at recess. He saw I was getting ahead a little, and he shouted, 'We shall see white black-birds after *you* get to the head.'"

"That's it," said Zeke. "There's always something at school or at home to trip us up, when we try to do anything. I do wish I could live one winter at Alden Farm. I kind of feel I should learn the secret of good luck."

"Well," replied Tom, a sudden and unusual inspiration coming over him, "Here's study this evening. I'll *make* luck at Crone's Corner."

The boys went with these feelings and took their usual place on blocks in one corner of the kitchen fire-place. Their sisters were seated in the other corner. The parents sat near the middle of the room, at the large stand, on which blazed the tallow candles. The girls were playing "puzzle" with a slate, and for once, peace and happiness reigned supreme in the household.

"How Zeke and Tom do study," whispered Jane to her sister. "What is a-going to happen?"

"I'll tell you," replied Betsey, "they are a-going to be somebody in school. That's what's the matter!"

Just at this state of affairs, Mrs. Crone suddenly thought of the Catechism.

"Jane!" she said, sharply, "did you get the Catechisms I sent you for to the parson's? Not one could I find in this house. There's never anything here when you want it."

Jane went to her satchel and brought the desired books.

"Come here, Zeke and Tom," she said, in a tone which implied either a duty neglected, or one to be required against which she expected a rebellion that she was prepared to put down by the force of arms, if necessary. The boys came forward like dogs to the master's lash, and the mother opened the books, gave one to each, saying, "There, boys, get sixteen pages of these answers; and don't you let me see any other book in your hands until you can say every word. Do you hear?"

Tom timidly suggested that he should lose his place at school if he did not get the lesson to be recited in the morning, and that he would get the Catechism afterwards.

"There, now," shouted the mother, "don't talk to me about losing your place; you're at the foot now, I'll warrant, where my children always are."

Jane started to her feet when she saw Tom's disappointed looks, and was about to say, "Tom is most to the head!" when her mother's foot came down with emphasis, as she said, in a harsh, commanding tone, "Not another word from any of you! Do as I bid you!"

The children obeyed doggedly. The mother resumed her work, muttering, "Strange that my children always will *compel* me to scold before they do as I bid them. They never do mind the first time they are spoken to."

While Mrs. Crone was thus attending to the religious instruction of the children, Mr. Crone was humming a tune and dividing his attention between the Farmer's Almanac and the milk score of some poor neighbors.

"I do wish you'd be still your buzzing, Mr. Crone; seems as if, between the children's fussing and your everlasting hum, I should go distracted."

Mr. Crone laid down his Almanac, folded his hands in moody silence. His clouded brow gave intimations that he might not continue perfectly amiable. The boys, thinking the storm was diverted from them, began to whisper together. Tom looked up the chimney to the bright stars, which seemed to look lovingly down upon him as if they would soothe his wounded spirits.

"I wish," he said to Zeke, in an undertone,—"I wish I was up among the stars. It must be warm up there, for our fire always sends its heat that way!"

"Nobody from this house will ever get so high," responded Zeke, bitterly.

"There, now, take *that*, and attend to your Catechism," exclaimed Mrs. Crone, coming suddenly upon the boys, as they were off their guard, and giving each a rousing box on the ear. "You think to whine round, by and by, and say you c-a-n-t g-e-t i-t! I'll teach you that I'm to be obeyed!"

The boys broke into an uncontrolable sobbing from mingled grief and vexation, and the girls began to cry from sympathy with their brothers.

"Jane," said Mrs. Crone, "take the candle, and do you and Betsey go to bed this minute, and let me hear no more from you to-night."

The girls went crying to bed, without any of the "Good night, mother, good night, all," or other sweet farewells, which make the departure of children to their slumbers like a pleasant song. Zeke and Tom continued a nervous sobbing, which their mother endeavored in vain to suppress. Worried out at last she drove them both to bed. No prayers were offered at their bed-side that night, but many muttered complaints, which gave evidence that they had been provoked to wrath, and were discouraged.

When the parents were alone, Mr. Crone remarked, with firmness, "Jerusha, you are too harsh with the children. You do them more hurt than good!"

"There, Ezekiel, that's just the way, if ever I try to do my duty to the children!" said Mrs. Crone, bursting into tears. Her loud sobbing prevented any further remark, except as she sobbed in broken sentences, "I never will try to do anything for them"— "I'm always blamed"—"I'll let it all go"— "I don't care if they never know a word of the Catechism"—"I'll tell everybody I have done *my* duty!"

So the parents followed the children to bed, under the same dark cloud which had made the night hideous to the whole household.

A sullen silence reigned in the family during the morning hours. The dog, as he looked in the faces of its members, skulked away under the settle, with drooping ears and tail, desiring but not daring to ask for his morning meal. The breakfast was swallowed, but not eaten. The family prayers were said, but not offered with the "heart's adoration." The old kitchen was like the deck of a vessel, which had been struck by the first gust of a tempest of drenching rain and terrific thunder, whose sailors waited in silence another shock. The boys went moping and crest-fallen to school, to fail in their lessons, go to the foot of their classes, and be taunted with belonging to "Crone's Corner." Mrs. Crone tossed the Catechisms into a dusty corner of the book-case, and for a week no reference was made to them by either parents or children. The boys were permitted to spend their evenings as they pleased, and, as their ambition for the school lessons was very low, time hung heavily on their hands. At the end of the week, under the promptings of Mr. Crone, the Catechisms were taken from the shelf and sleepily studied for a few evenings, when the old kitchen witnessed another gale. The wind blew this time from another quarter, but the desolate track which it left was equally marked.

"Mr. Crone!" said his wife, one evening, breaking the painful silence which reigned in the family circle, by an equally painful tone of voice.

Mr. Crone raised his eyes from his score-book with an expression of indifference to whatever might be said.

"Mr. Crone," continued the wife, "do you know that I am working myself almost to death, while these lazy boys are hanging about the house, doing nothing half of the time?"

"You get some help from Jane," suggested Mr. Crone.

"Jane!" replied Mrs. Crone, with an expressive sneer; "a child but nine years old, and feeble thing too, as you know. There's Alden's boys, they do all his wife's work, I'm told, while she plays the lady. My boys are none too good to help their mother, and they *shall* do it."

Mrs. Crone now "pitched in" to the boys, assigning to Zeke, the older son, certain days in which he was to scrub the floor, and to Tom his time and turn in helping Jane wash the dishes.

The spirit of this requirement, more than the work to be done, came in contact with what little religious benefit the boys were getting from the Catechism. They obeyed the distasteful command, for, as they said, "While mother's temper is up, it won't answer not to mind." But there is an obedience by children, which, in its spirit and manner, is the most sinful kind of disobedience. So it was in this case. Tom's hands, in washing the dishes, so sympathized with his unwilling heart, that he often dropped and broke them. His eyes too came in for a part in the plot against the right performance of the task, and refused to see the dirt upon the plates which should have been washed off.

Zeke declared that when he would do right, blunders were present with him. He upset pails of water most unfortunately for the advancement of the cleaning. There were no songs in this night of the children's trouble, and no stories to beguile the slowly moving time. The spirit of bitter words were not applied to the tedious moments, but to the burdens of the heart, and increased them.

The boys who came to invite the young Crones to play with them, learned how they were employed, and taunted them, by calling them "girl-boys," and "old grannies." Some boys are like wolves; if one of their companions is faint or lame, they fall upon and devour him. This was adding insult to injury, and Zeke and Tom, "pitched in," as boys now-a-days say, and a fight was the consequence, which, of course, resulted in an increase of the bad reputation of the boys of Crone's Corner.

There soon came an evening when the wayward working of the children was too much for the endurance of the mother. She drove them both from the room, saying, "There, go! and don't you ever let me see you put your finger to anything in the kitchen again."

She returned to her work, muttering desponding words about her bad luck. "I might have known," she said, "that *I* should have got no help. There's Alden's wife! Oh, yes, *she* need only lift her finger and there's a plenty to serve; but I must drudge forever!" Mrs. Crone found relief to her wounded feelings in tears.

CHAPTER IV.

THE CHILDREN'S MEETING.

It was a clear, cold, winter day, on which the children of the parish of the Rev. Charles Curtis were to repair to the parsonage to recite the lessons of the Catechism, and to receive his promptings in understanding the way of salvation. The icy pearls on the trees and shrubs sparkled in the rays of the unclouded sun, and the sleigh runners creaked over the frosty snow. The girls, in their homespun dresses, with work-bags on their arms, and mittens on their hands of the grandmother pattern, whose ruddy faces were nearly hid in their warm hoods, looked as lovely, we doubt not, in the eyes of affectionate parents, and as bewitching in the estimation of the boys, as any modern-dressed misses. As to the boys, a farmer's frock, clean and warm, heavy cowhide boots, a strong arm, an honest and intelligent face, and hearts ever ready to dare and to do in the path of duty, made up the features of manly beauty which only fools despise.

Alden Farm was represented by five children,—Ruth, who was prompt in the assurance of ten pages of the Catechism; and Rachel, who could answer the questions of six pages; and little Jeremiah, who hugged his Primer as he trudged bravely behind his sisters, his heart swelling with an honest pride at the thought of what *he* could do; and, leading these three, Carver and Miles, who felt that they could "run through a troop or leap over a wall." A stranger, looking into the faces of this group of children, would see at a glance, an expression of real satisfaction in the expected meeting.

"Hurrah, Miles!" shouted Carver, as they

approached the parsonage, "there's Squire True's sleigh in the yard! yes, and Deacon Turner's too! Won't it be a good time!"

"I wonder, now," replied Miles, dryly, "if the Squire and the deacon know the Catechism! Let's examine them, Carver! I guess father and mother can beat both of them."

The children laughed at their brother's pleasantry. Jeremiah pulled Miles' coat, and looking innocently into his face, asked, "Will 'oo ask 'em real hard questions?"

Rachel said that they were real good men, and she was glad they were at the children's meeting.

The children of Alden Farm walked into the ample kitchen of the parsonage, with a quiet self-possession which wreathed their faces with smiles, and made the faces of all about them look pleasant. Jerry immediately made the acquaintance of the dog, which was watching with curious eyes the unusual stir, from his position under his master's great arm-chair. He was decidedly pleased to be noticed, and the two were soon very "thick."

"In good season, children," said the pastor, as he passed hastily through the kitchen, to usher in other company. "In good season, just as the Alden Farm people are at church."

Let us leave this happy company, and look down the road toward Crone's Corner. Two boys are creeping along at a snail's pace. They stop once in a while, as if in debate whether to come on or to return. There is no particular fault in their personal appearance. Their mother, Mrs. Crone, is, as we have seen, a hard working woman, and has both energy and good sense in providing her childen's clothes. So Zeke and Tom, who are the boys whom we see down the road, are not feeling "put down" by not being dressed as well as most others. Their mother has driven them out to the parsonage gathering, to show that she has done her duty, even if they do, when there, "make fools of themselves." We have seen the training for the occasion which they have had, so they drag themselves reluctantly towards the parsonage, as a sick and over-burdened laborer, goaded by the necessities of a starving family, returns to his daily task.

As they approached the yard, Zeke exclaimed with a rueful countenace, "Tom, Squire True and Deacon Turner are there! See, there's their sleigh!"

"I won't go!" exclaimed Tom, bursting into tears. "I guess I won't make a fool of myself before all the parish, if mother don't care!"

Both boys paused again, to renew their courage, as a panting horse does his strength, by "stopping to blow." Slowly they entered the yard, and stood partly hid by a woodpile, watching the happy troop of children as they filed in. Tom kicked the snow with his boot, mostly eyeing, in a listless manner, the chips and dirt which he turned up from beneath.

"See!" said Parson Curtis, looking from the window, "there stand the Crone children. Why don't they come in?"

"Poor fellows!" said Deacon Turner, seizing his hat and going to the door.

"Boys," said the deacon, in a kind tone, "we are glad to see you. You are a little bashful, I see. No bad sign either, in these days when so many young folks are older and bolder than their parents. Come, your pastor will be glad to see you."

The boys followed him into the house with a confidence which surprised themselves.

"This way, Ezekiel and Thomas," said the pastor, pointing to two chairs which he had set for them in a corner, where they would least feel the presence of the company. "A little timid, I see," he whispered, smiling as they sat down. "But that is a fault which the children lose in my great kitchen."

"It's a fact, Tom," said Zeke, in a low tone. "I'm losing my scare!"

Zeke fairly straightened up in his chair, as he said this, and even Tom looked squarely into his pastor's face as he began to speak a word of welcome to all; seeing only kindness expressed there, he ventured to turn his eyes to the faces of Squire True and Deacon Turner. The light of Christian love which beamed from them, fell upon the disheartened boy as sunbeams fall on the drooping flower. His own countenance began to reflect the good feeling which pervaded the company.

After a prayer by Parson Curtis, and a song by all, the recitations commenced, the entire knowledge of the Catechism of each one being thoroughly but kindly drawn out. Whether by accident or design, no one knew; but the Alden Farm children were the first who were called out. Seeing that they answered the questions so promptly, the pastor proposed a few questions concerning the meaning of the great truths taught.

"It's wonderful that those children understand such things so well!" whispered the deacon to Squire True.

"Not at all wonderful, deacon," replied the squire. "Don't you see John and Patience Alden in the eyes of their children — I mean the religious spirit of the parents beaming in their children's countenances?"

The deacon nodded assent.

"What a stupid show we shall make, Tom," whispered Zeke, the old discouragement coming over him.

"Let's creep out," replied Tom.

But the sober, second thought, held them in their seats. The examination went on, and the Crones began to breathe more freely.

"Zeke," said Tom, looking several inches taller than he had done since the reciting commenced, "I can do as well as that!"

A boy of Tom's age had just sat down.

Partly from a neglect of his lesson, and partly through bashfulness, he blundered badly. But somehow, none of the children knew exactly how, their minister made every blunderer feel ashamed of present deficiency, and a secret resolution to do better next time, without exciting discouragement or ill-feeling. When he came to the Crones, this wisdom and tact seemed to be in its fullest exercise. They both saw and felt their great deficiency, but there was no bitterness attending the feeling.

"What surprising success our minister has on these occasions!" said Squire True, in an under-tone. "What can be the secret of it, deacon?"

"It's the Christ-spirit in him," said the deacon warmly. "He does so *love* the children!"

When the examination was over, and the deacon and squire had added words in full sympathy with those of their pastor, and God's blessing had been asked, to rest upon all the lambs of the flock, an hour of social interview was spent. Apples were passed round among the children, and restraint and stiffness disappeared. The pastor's wife, and his daughter, Miss Jane Curtis, about fifteen years old, were in every part of the company, in turn, carrying good words to all. The deacon and the squire were young in heart. For the time every child seemed as one of their own family. They proved, as the inner life of thousands of our Puritan fathers has proved, that the sourness of spirit sometimes attributed to them, is simply a slander. These two Puritans were like most others, stern and exacting in what they deemed great principles, but genial and loving in their social relations.

Ezekiel and Thomas Crone came out of their corner, early in the social interview. They ate their share of the apples, did a full part in the talking, and more than their part in the laughing. They were, in fact, happy beyond any former experience.

"Tom," exclaimed Zeke, as soon as they were on the way home, "we have had a good time!"

"Young man!—Mr. Ezekiél Crone, I mean," replied Tom, stopping and drawing himself up to his full height, "we have had a *splendid* time."

"I'll bet," replied Zeke, "that I'll know every word in that big little book, next time!"

Tom did not hear this last declaration, but it expressed his own purpose; he had started for home in a full run. The boys reached Crone's Corner, out of breath with running, and in fine spirits. They spoke of the visit to the parsonage in glowing language. "Why," said Zeke, "Deacon Turner and Squire True talked more with us than they did with any of the boys; they were most as good as our minister; and Miss Jane told us that her father and all her folks would have been real disappointed if we had not come."

Sunshine prevailed for a while even in the kitchen of the Crones. Kind words and deeds at the parsonage had given them an almost unexperienced inspiration towards good luck. The boys once more pored over their school books, and studied slyly, but diligently, their Catechisms. When their mother saw the favorable change, she remarked to her husband, complacently, "Ezekiel, I am glad I persevered and did my duty to the children about the Catechism. You see what the result is."

Her husband looked provokingly stupid, as if he did not quite see the point, while Mrs. Crone proceeded, "If our minister knew how hard I worked to bring about the interest in religious things he must see in our boys, and he knew too, how little help I had from anybody, he would give me more credit than he does now."

Mr. Crone remained an unappreciative listener to these delicate claims, and she dropped the subject by remarking, quite as much to herself as to her husband, "It would be entirely too much good luck for me to have any good done in my family, and to get the credit of it too."

CHAPTER V.

THE RAISING.

We must pass in silence other important events of "the Farm," and of "the Corner," which occurred during the winter of which we have been speaking.

An event of interest took place at Crone's Corner in the early part of the following summer. The crops were well started. The mowing had not commenced. Ezekiel Crone had been hard at work during the winter. He was, it must be remembered, a hard-working, honest man; and his wife, let it not be forgotten, was a woman of industry and management. Well, Ezekiel had attended, during the winter, with such help as he received from his boys, to all the barn work; cut and brought to the door a large supply of wood for the summer; carried out manure upon his grass land; and had cut, hewn and framed the material for an addition to his barn. During the spring, as other work allowed, he had drawn to the saw-mill logs to be sawed into boards for the floors and covering. "A raising!" was already whispered among the young people of the town, while the logs lay waiting their turn at the saw-mill. George Parsons, the kind-hearted man who tended the saw, spoke a good word for Ezekiel to all comers.

"Neighbors," he would say, "Ezekiel isn't as thrifty as some, but he has got together, by hard work, a fairish kind of addition for his barn. Come to the raising and give him a lift."

"We must go to Zeke's raising," said the loungers about the tavern and grocery store. "He's not one of your mean fellows. He will have plenty of good liquors."

"We must help Brother Crone," remarked Deacon Turner, as he passed the Corner one day, and observed the increasing piles of lumber. "He does seem to have a large number of head flaws in life. Some men seem to be born to it. I must be at the raising."

"Now, Ezekiel," said Mrs. Crone, the day before the raising was to come off, "the men who came to our last raising made a great noise about my premises, and made me a great deal of trouble. I do believe I worked harder in getting them lunches, than any man at the building. You know that I am willing to work just as hard again as you do, but as to doing all the treating, I shan't do it."

"I have engaged a good supply of rum," said Ezekiel, quietly.

"Well, I do desire you wouldn't be mean with it, for the Crones must supply double to what rich folks would, in order to satisfy people. The mercy knows I hope nobody will take too much, but *our* building will never go up without a good supply."

"That's what I think," said Mr. Crone.

"And you can sweep a clean place in the barn, make a table of some of your new, clean boards, and put the drink and bread and cheese upon it. It will be handy, and everybody shall have all they want, and not plague me in my kitchen. If the men do come bothering round they'll learn that Jerusha Crone knows how to teach 'em manners."

"You will have a pot of coffee ready for those who prefer it," suggested Ezekiel.

"Not I!" replied Mrs. Crone, decidedly. "Nobody but an old Betty wants coffee on such an occasion. The men will have plenty of rum, and that's enough. You are always planning to make work for me."

Ezekiel said no more. The clean place in the barn was prepared. The table was spread with an abundance of fresh bread and "good old cheese." To the credit of Mrs. Crone, it ought to be said, that her bread was excelled by that of no wife in town; and to the discredit of the age, it may be stated that the liquor, which, as Mr. Crone had promised, was also abundant, was the vilest of drinks, though in this respect, it is no doubt far excelled by the poisonous compounds of our present liquor shops.

The day of raising came. Neighbors and towns-people were not backward in the customary good will offering of their services. The Crones had no reason to complain that the people turned their backs on *their* necessities.. It being Saturday, the children were also present in great numbers.

"We'll have to wet a little before this hard work begins," said a stout young man of 28 years.

"Zeke's none of your mean fellows," said another, as a generous glass of rum went to his mouth.

The barn table, at least the end supporting the drink, was thus well visited before the work commenced.

"Men," said Squire True, as he held up an exceedingly moderate glass of liquor in the sight of the crowd, "I hope no man will take too much to-day. It is a shame to do so. Yes, I do not hesitate to say it is a great sin. The good things of God should not be abused."

Having delivered this temperance speech, the squire swallowed his moderate glass of rum.

The deacon — Deacon Turner — then gave his solemn warning against drunkenness, and wound up by taking a *very* moderate glass. Neither the squire nor the deacon touched another drop while at the Corner. They had come mainly to give the occasion the moral benefit of their example, and to show their good will towards Mr. Crone. They were ready also to see that the carpenter's orders were carried out by the men.

Frames in these days were substantial affairs. They did not consist, as now, in pieces of lumber which two men may take up easily, and with the assistance of a third one, put into almost any part of a first class house. Mechanical aid was almost unknown. Heavy timbers went into their places by the power of muscles. But this was not the worst of the bad management of the builders. It was thought necessary to put a section of a frame together, and thus to lift it into its place. Long and heavy poles were used with an iron point. When the frame was lifted from the floor, these, handled by as many men as could get hold, were braced against it, and with vociferous shouting, the side of the building was lifted into its place. Strong men stood at the mortises with iron bars, to keep the tenons from slipping, and to send them into their places.

With as much bustle as would occur to launch a modern ship of twelve hundred tons, the men laid hold of the first section of the frame. It was started from the floor by main strength, the "proppers" keeping what was gained until the "spike poles" were struck into it, and by a strong push altogether, the tenons settled into the mortises, and so much of the work was done.

That part of the company which had the weakness of taking a "*leetle*" too much, visited the table at the barn for a bit of bread and cheese, and something to wash it down. Thus the work went on, until the frame which supported the scaffold floor was in its place.

"Well done, men," said Squire True; "steady, now, and drink *very moderately*, and neighbor Crone's barn is all right."

"It's all owing to plenty of good liquor," said a tavern lounger. "Zeke Crone's cordials make us as strong as giants."

The scaffold floor was laid, and the first heavy section of the frame which bore the plates upon which the rafters were to be adjusted, was lifted upon the props. The "spike poles" were thrust against it, and it was raised about half way to its place, when a recruit of four men coming late from the barn table, strong as giants from liberal potations of the "cordial," seized a pole and made a desperate and sudden push upon the frame. Their jerk loosened the hold of full half of the other poles, and they fell to the floor. This left the whole weight of the frame upon those who were straining at the few remaining poles.

"Stand from under!" shouted Squire True, as he seized one of the drunken men, and thrust him out of harm's way. Before the fallen poles could come to the rescue, the strength of the men holding the others was gone.

"Stand from under!" was again shouted, as the frame came to the floor with a crash. The tenons and braces were broken, making work for the carpenters, before any further raising could be done. But this was a small part of the accident. Mr. Crone's foot slipped as he let go, and he fell backwards. One end of the pole fell upon his leg, as the other end came under the full weight of the descending timber. He was immediately extricated, but his piteous groaning, too well assured the men even before the doctor declared the fact, that his leg was broken.

Mrs. Crone's energy and efficient help rose superior, for the time, to all complaining. No person of the whole company showed more coolness. The sufferer was soon in a quiet chamber, his leg set and "splintered," and his mind left to its reflection, and his family to a conviction of the "summer's task" which was before them.

The raisers scattered, each with his remarks, and all with a sincere regret for the accident, and sympathy for the suffering family.

"The fools must give out and let their spike poles drop, when smart men gave the frame a touch," said the drunkards, somewhat sobered now and feeling conscious that they had caused the accident. "If *all* had taken a bumber of Crone's cordial, and not the stingy bit which Deacon Turner preached up, we'd pushed the plaguy thing into the middle of next week, and Zeke's leg wouldn't have been broke. It's all owing to the deacon's and the squire's temp'rance nonsense."

There was, that evening, an earnest talk at the parsonage. Deacon Turner and the squire, made their pastor an early call to talk over the serious event of the day. While these three were in the midst of their discussion, Doctor Burt came in. The doctor was the wisest man of the age — in his own estimation; and this claim was disputed by the people in favor of their minister only. To blister, bleed, give "blue pills, salts and senna," with ardent spirit, "*quan-*

tum sufficit," was the chief end of the physician's calling, in his estimation; and to submit to his treatment, the chief end of man.

"This whole trouble has come," the squire and deacon affirmed with one voice, "because the men did not heed our solemn warning, and our faithful example, concerning the use of ardent spirit. They took too much, and God's judgment came upon their sin."

The doctor gave a complacent nod. If the people, he said, would only take his advice, all would be well. He had, through his long, as he trusted, not altogether unsuccessful practice, commanded all men everywhere not to exceed three drams a day, except by his special permission.

Mr. Curtis, the pastor, made but few remarks. His distinguished callers were surprised at his unusual silence. The doctor was slightly offended that he did not express admiration at his modest claims, and profound suggestions. The more discerning deacon perceived that his pastor's spirits were stirred within him, and that his musings were foreshadowing some new course of thought and duty. This the deacon *thought* he perceived, and even the doctor, before retiring, indulged suspicions, and shook his head the next time he met the squire, saying, "I fear our good pastor is going to take some unwise measure in reference to the little indiscretions of the men at the late raising." He always, patronizingly called Mr. Curtis "our *good* pastor," when he wished to show his own superior wisdom.

Whether the doctor and the deacon rightly discerned the thoughts of their pastor, we shall see.

CHAPTER VI.

MORE LUCK AT ALDEN FARM.

Ezekiel Crone had been sleeping uneasily, when he turned his face towards the chair in which his wife, for the last twenty-four hours, had been almost constantly sitting. He was about to say, "Jerusha, you had better lie down and get a little sleep. You'll be sick, then what will become of us?" But his eyes met those of Patience Alden, who had, during his sleep, come in, sent his wife to bed, and taken her place as a watcher. Hope and courage came to the suffering man, from the expression of her face. A few days later, he learned that John Alden and his boys, with a company of townsmen of his selecting, had been at the Corner, repaired damages, finished raising the barn, and put other friends in the way of its completion. This was not all. When Ezekiel was able to sit up, and look out upon his mowing land, a surprise was planned for him. He expected to see his grass "lodged" and spoiled, his crops overrun with weeds, and a dismal look all about, for the next winter. But the last of his hay, all well made, was just entering his barn. His boys, instead of lounging, seemed full of work. His garden never looked finer. His corn and potatoes sent pleasant greetings by the passing breeze, to their owner at the window, assuring him of their most excellent health.

The invalid buried his face in his hands, and bowed his head upon the window sill, weeping freely, as he murmured softly, "I see how it is. John Alden and his boys have been round."

The harvest weeks were just setting in, when Mr. Crone, with nearly his usual strength, returned to his labor. His granaries promised to be quite as full as usual. His sons, Zeke and Tom, appeared to him "a head taller and a deal smarter" than in the spring.

The case of the Crones was in discussion at this time, during the intermission on Sunday, by a company of men who were eating their lunch in the horse-sheds. They were not of the baser sort, but substantial heads of families.

The hour between the morning and afternoon service, and the horse-sheds and the environs of the church, were to our fathers in the rural districts in olden times, and down to the formation of Sunday Schools, institutions of no small educating power. Then and there the passing events and current questions in state and church were discussed, neighborhood matters talked over, while frugal lunches were eaten.

At the time of which we are speaking,

George Parsons, of the saw-mill, introduced the subject. "It is surprising, certainly, friends," he remarked, as a generous piece of rye bread waited between his fingers to stop his mouth by going in, "it is surprising how John Alden accomplishes so much. He and his boys have, this past summer, done most of the work of two farms. Yes, friends, and let me tell you that the old farm at the Corners never smiled so upon its owner as now."

"It don't signify," said a gray headed old man, giving his clean Sunday frock a vigorous twitch, "John Alden is *jest a leetle* too zealous. I'm told, but I'm not sartin though that it's true, that Zeke Crone had taken a bit too much when he broke his leg. If so, he was sarved right. I hold that every man's got enough to do to take care of his own farm, and nobody's called to work for them who don't know how to stop drinking when they've got enough."

The horse-shed circle agreed with the old man, for they held that gray hairs *did* teach wisdom — that is, when they uttered words which they approved.

But Alden Farm gave the town another theme over which there was much wonder and talk. "A raising" had come off there. It was not generally known that any was in preparation. But the preparations had been so quietly made, and when the frame was ready, the building had been so quietly and quickly put up, that some fairy seemed to have come to the place, smiled upon John and Patience, spoken kindly to the children, and then, to show the approval of all fairies of the good deeds of the summer, waved her wand, and brought up the building. But the locality of our story is in plain, matter-of-fact New England, where there are no fairies. So we must explain what the new building was, and how it came into existence.

It was not a great affair, but simply a long, wide shed, connecting the house with the barn. Its posts were of a good height, and, by all precedent, it was fairly entitled to a raising. The lumber required was nearly equal in its number of square feet, to the new barn at Crone's Corner. Its material was the result of odd hours of work for several winters, and had been "sticked up," in the old shed, out of sight. The framing had been done there. When John Alden saw the results of the raising at Crone's, he and Patience took the whole subject of raisings and their attending "treating" into serious discussion. Long and earnestly did they look at the subject, and as they turned it over, and sharply examined it, it grew in breadth and importance. One fact in connection with dram drinking appeared to them as it never had done before. It was the effect of it upon the boys and young men. This was impressed upon them by an incident at the late raising, which but few had noticed. It was this,—Crone's boys were drunk on the evening of the accident. They had, in common with other boys, sipped the rum and sugar from the bottom of the tumblers used by the raisers. On the sudden leaving of the men, "more than was good for them" was left to their share. In the confusion from the broken leg, little notice was taken of them, and only sharp observers like John Alden had noticed their condition.

"Think of my boys drunk!" said John, during one of the kitchen evening discussions with Patience. And he arose from the stand, and walked the floor in an excitement quite rare with him.

"Think of *my husband* a drunkard!" responded Patience, without raising her eyes from the little frock of one of the girls, which she was patching.

This was another nail in a sure place.

John paused, looked earnestly into Patience's serious, calm face, and, after a few moments' silence, said, slowly, "Why not John Alden a drunkard? Many better men have been conquered by the demon Alcohol. I will never taste the ruinous stuff again!"

"Nor provide it for others," said Patience, in the same calm, quiet tone, with a shade more of emphasis than before.

"Patience," said John, sitting down, and resting his elbow upon the stand, and reaching forward until his face came almost in contact with that of his wife's. A looker-on might have supposed he was about to kiss her, nor are we quite sure that he did not. "Patience, you are always a little ahead of me in every right path. But how shall we get along in haying time when I have to call upon my neighbors to give me a good turn, as some dark cloud threatens to pour its contents upon my well made hay? how, when I want men to go logging with me in the winter,—how at the expected raising?"

These were questions like many others, which are old now, but were then just occupying the minds of a few only—the few whose hearts and minds God had touched.

Patience lifted her eyes from her work and set them full upon John. Her cheeks were slightly flushed with the blush he had just excited. Never, not even when she blushingly said, "I will," in the marriage vow, had she seemed so loveable in his eyes. "What shall we do, John? do right, and trust in God!"

All discussion on the subject was ended from that time. A sweet peace settled down upon John Alden, unknown before even to him, in his moments of greatest nearness to God. He was now, in heart and practice, a "teetotaler." "Do right, and trust in God!" They were words which involved an old, not a new obligation. But they fell upon John Alden like words in prophetic vision, upon the old seers. The candles upon the stand seemed to blaze with a brighter, purer flame, as if appointed of God to symbolize the increased spiritual light granted to his servants. Such illuminations of the spirit as John and Patience Alden now experienced, does God give to those who seek, as they did, in persistent faith and prayer, to know and do his whole will.

These statements explain why John Alden's raising went up so quietly and privately. He went to a number sufficient for his purpose, of friends most likely to respond to his remarkable request. "Come, neighbors," he said, in his outspoken way, "I have a bit of a frame which I want to put up. I shan't wet it with a drop of liquor. If you can trust John Alden for a good turn in the same way, come on. If not, don't come." Every man who was invited came,— came early, all worked with a will and without bluster, and the work was done, and nobody drank anything stronger than Patience Alden's coffee. All returned home when the work was done, profoundly respecting John Alden, although some criticised sharply his new notions.

When Jerusha Crone heard of this affair, she burst into tears. She "couldn't help it," she said. Not that she envied such "a dear good man" as John Alden. "But there it is," she said. "John Alden can have help without its costing him a cent. He needn't give them a drop of anything, when our liquor cost us dollars and dollars, and then—. I don't like to complain of my Maker, and I won't,"—and she broke out afresh in sobs and tears, as she added, "but my dear, honest husband must have a leg broke, and we get nothing but failure and blame."

So it was, there was no "luck" at Crone's Corner, except what the kindness of its friends carried there! How strange! thought its suffering victims. But perhaps our secret may be known sometime, to even them.

Though John Alden's shed had gone up quietly, its manner of raising produced a decided breeze. Dr. Burt learned with indignation, the stand which Alden Farm folks had taken. He resolved himself at once into a committee to wait upon them. He considered his wisdom called in question by a plain, unlearned farmer. It would never do, for he had maintained all his life that moderate drinking was a virtue, and excess was a great crime.

"I have called, sir," said the doctor, addressing John Alden, "to give you my professional opinion in the matter of the use and abuse of alcoholic drinks."

While delivering this message, the doctor assumed his most imposing air. The knowing nod of his head at its close, said, "*I, wisdom, teach knowledge.*" He had come, after a slight knock, which he did not wait to have answered, into the kitchen. John stood in the middle of the floor, in his farmer's frock, milk-pail in hand. His heavy cowhide boots gave him a firm footing upon the floor. The well-developed muscles of his arm, and the labor-worn hardness of his fist, might well have intimidated an ordinary man, if there had been any occasion to fear their violent use. As the doctor ended the abrupt announcement of his business, a close observer might have seen a slight and furtive contraction of Alden's brow, indicating defiance and angry words. But even an indifferent by-stander could see the straightening up of his manly form, and the unconscious moving forward of his right foot. In a deep, steady voice, in which there was the steady force of a sea captain on the quarter-deck in a storm, who is conscious that he is master of the situation, John Alden said, "Doctor, when we are sick in body, and can't get along with Patience's remedies and good nursing, we call the doctor; when we are sick in heart, or perplexed concerning

Patience, flat-iron in hand, calmly surveyed the doctor. Page 89.

duty, *we go to another source altogether.*" The last sentence was uttered with an emphasis to which John's cowhide boot gave force, by a slight rise and sudden descent upon the kitchen floor. The man of pretentious learning wilted before the honest yeoman of common sense. To add to his confusion, Patience, who had continued at her ironing till just at this crisis, turned round, flat-iron in hand, and calmly surveyed the doctor. John had set his milk-pail down, folded his arms across his breast, and was awaiting, like a giant clad in mail, his opponent's assault.

The doctor fluttered from his boots to his hair, like a ship's sails out of which the wind had been suddenly taken, and stammered out, "But, well, you'll argue this matter — it's a great question."

"Patience and I have argued and settled it," said John, waving his hand triumphantly towards his wife, as a victorious general would turn to his chief of staff by whom he had conquered.

"Settled it, without consulting your pastor or"—

"Yes," interposed Alden, in a voice which began to assume a tone of authority, "settled it, sir, without consulting the minister or doctor!" Then, dropping his voice into a tender, solemn utterance, as he stepped forward and put his mouth almost to the doctor's ear, he said, "Yes, Patience and I *settled it*, after consulting,—on our knees in secret, and at the family altar, the All-Wise. And, doctor, it *is* settled! I will never, *never* touch alcoholic drink again. I will *never* again put the cup to my neighbor's lips!"

The doctor stooped and took up his hat which had dropped upon the floor, and turned to leave.

"Doctor," said Patience, with one of her sweetest smiles, "stop and take tea with us.

You do not often favor us with a friendly call."

"Do," added John,—"and take a farmer's fare and a farmer's welcome. There are none better!"

But the doctor beat a retreat with an awkward apology, after having shown a decided inclination to tarry any length of time to "argue." He continued to denounce the Alden Farm "ultraism," but he was never known to allude to the fact that he had made John Alden a call on the subject.

Soon after, John and Patience received visitors of a different spirit. They were Deacon Turner and Squire True. They came in no blustering spirit, but as brethren of the same church communion. They said they had heard of the decided stand Mr. Alden had taken for the elevation of the moral standard in the town, with much pleasure. But they were afraid he was going too far. They feared hurt might be done to the holy cause of temperance by so strenuous a demand as that of denying the moderate use of liquor on suitable occasions.

John's vigorous common sense drove through their objections to his position, like a fifty horse power engine through a snow bank. He left, too, a straight and clean track behind him, to show what he had done.

After a friendly chat of an hour, the deacon turned to his companion, and remarked pleasantly, "Squire, you see these people have fully made up their mind concerning this matter. I think we have no further duty here."

"Yes," replied the squire, "but perhaps brother Alden has a further duty in reference to us. Speak on, neighbor Alden, I can hear more."

John then closed the talk with an account of his remarkable experience when his final decision was made.

"We came to reprove and convict of error," remarked the squire, as they slowly walked away. "But I think, Brother Turner, we return almost persuaded of the wisdom of John's way."

"You speak my mind," said the deacon.

The quiet of Alden Farm was undisturbed by the commotion it had caused in the town. It fact, its unpretending family were unconscious of having caused any commotion. They builded better than they knew. They seriously had asked God to show them the right way, and, having learned it, walked unflinchingly in it.

"John Alden," said Mrs. Crone, "cares for nobody, and does as he's a mind to. I'll warrant our great folks — the deacon and the squire, and maybe the parson, will praise him for it yet. *If I* do as I'm a mind to, I'm a stubborn, wicked women, folks say, at once, and some judgment, like a broken leg, lights upon me right off. It does seem strange! But I never did have any good luck."

"John Alden is stingy," said the tavern loafers. "He won't treat at a raising. I'll wager that his shed will tumble down. No building can stand that goes up without liquor."

"Alden's a mean nobody," responded the bar-keeper.

"He makes a plaguy fuss in this heer town for a nobody," hiccoughed a half tipsy customer. "It's my opinion, gentlemen, that John Alden's a pretty tolerable, decent sort of a man, and that he could buy and keep on hand the whole of ye."

The pastor, Mr. Curtis, watched and studied the turn things were taking. He was a cautious, decided, honest man. He was slow to act in new movements, but unselfish and unshrinking when the path of duty was plain. Somehow, though both stood in independent positions, the lights of Alden Farm and the parsonage seemed ever blending together.

CHAPTER VII.

THE HUSKING.

It happened with John Alden's townpeople that one theme of gossip lasted until another occurred. His "raising" was talked about until his "husking" came off. So generous had he been with his time in the interest of others, that his unusually large crop of corn remained in the field until the November snow began to fall. Other work would soon crowd upon him, while the barn floor contained a most discouraging heap which waited for the huskers.

"Father," said Carver, "Miles and I think our winter school will begin before that corn is out of the barn floor. Can't we have a husking?"

The boy's mother had been asking, "Can't we have a husking?" and all the children took up the question. The huskings, up to that time, had been, as almost every special occasion for the people to gather together had been, a time of "treating." With many, the drinking had been the principal attraction. Could there be a husking without strong drink? was John Alden's query. He had squarely decided that if there could not, he would husk his own corn, though it lay in the barn embarrassing his other work until spring. He had proved that a small building, at least, could be raised without it. But a husking was in a marked degree, a social gathering, and it would, he thought, be considered very unsocial without strong drink.

As was his custom in every perplexity, he talked the matter over with Patience.

"Had we not, Patience," he suggested, "in view of the opposition to our stand against strong drink, try to get along alone with the husking?"

"The children's school begins next week," said Patience. "Their time for study must not be embarrassed. The chores will be all the boys can do. Your work in the woods begins soon. Besides, John, there is good to be done *just now* by a husking."

"Will you explain," said John, "how that can be?"

"Why, look here, John," replied Patience, with a glance of surprise, "it will give us a chance to declare more publicly our principles. If they are right, we should publish them abroad. *I feel just like doing it.*"

John smiled at his wife's zeal, and gave his vote for a husking.

"I guess it will be a good time," said Miles. To this the younger children gave assent by their overflow of good spirits. Even baby Winslow was informed that a great amount of fun was in store for him, and Rachel gravely imformed him that he could not have "one drop of *toddy*," to which little Jerry added the wise and important explanation that "it is not good for 'oo."

The Crones heard of the husking to come off at the Alden Farm, with their usual feeling of mingled wonder, doubt and envy, at the proposals from that quarter.

"John will be lucky," said Mr. Crone, "if he gets that big heap of corn husked without paying for or using any liquor."

"Of course he will," said Mrs. Crone. "Folks'll run to John's. He has a knack of making 'em do so."

The Crone children discussed the matter in their way.

"Zeke," said Tom, "it will be a dry old time at Alden Farm next Wednesday night; a big heap of corn to husk, and no rum and sugar in the bottoms of the tumblers."

"That is so; a dry, mean old time," responded Zeke.

A pause of a moment followed, which Tom broke with an exclamation of great energy for him. "Zeke, let's go!"

"Agreed!" shouted Zeke, jumping up and striking his cowhide boots together as he came down upon the barn floor. Tom attested his joy at the anticipated "dry old time," by tossing his fur cap into the air, and kicking it as it came down, with such vigor, that it lodged on the hay mow.

There was, *somehow*, an attraction about all that was going on at Alden Farm, which made the children of the parish want to go, though their "notions" were sneered at by both old and young. Some of the old folks went so far as to say that if Patience Alden should send out word to the young folks to come to Alden Farm to be whipped all round, they would go, for they would say, "Aunt Patience's love will more'n pay for the rods."

We cannot say whether this was so or

not, but we know that "young America" of those times, "loved dearly" to go to all gatherings at John Alden's.

The husking afternoon arrived. At an early hour the people came in large numbers. The young people were largely represented. Even Mr. and Mrs. Crone could not see their children go without accompanying them. The hard drinking loungers of the tavern and stores, came late and slyly. They had first secured a stiff glass of rum and molasses, in view of John Alden's expected stinginess in this direction. William Treat and Moses Pond were representative men of this class. They passed on ahead of their companions "to explore the coast," as they said, while their companions sat down in a turn of the road, a few rods from the premises.

"Look here, Mose," said Treat, in a whisper, as he pushed open the door of the new shed, and peered at its contents, "look here, I say, Mose."

Moses Pond crept softly to the shed door, took a deliberate survey of its contents.

"Whew!" said Mose, in an undertone, "let's go to the husking!"

Moses slipped into the barn among the huskers, while Treat returned to his companions to report concerning the appearance of things.

"Men!" he exclaimed, like one amazed, "Aunt Patience has set a table clear'n the whole length of the new shed. Her table cloths are as white as old maid Crone's, who's been known to chase a fly a half a day in summer, rather'crn to have one in her kitchen. Then you ought to see what she's got on it! Such punk'in pies! and such poodens! I smelled the tea and coffee too, and they set me right up. They's got the real Java, and no mistake; and I shouldn't wonder if the tea was the real 'old hisin.' Men, let's go to John Alden's huskin'."

To this all agreed, but several of them

slyly peered into the new shed to assure themselves that there could be an attractive looking table without alcohol.

The half drunken men pushed open the barn door and stepped in. At the first sight of the huskers, they involuntarily paused and stood confused. A profusion of light blazed upon the company from lanterns suspended over their heads. Parson Curtis, and the leading members of his flock, were there. The young people — the girls and the boys — were present in great numbers. John Alden was in his happiest mood, taking away the rapidly filled baskets of yellow corn, and watching to secure for all comfortable positions near the diminishing heap.

The face of Patience Alden glowed with animation. She seemed free from care, as if the successful conducting of this enterprise, in which a great moral reform was concerned, was no responsibility of hers. Like a skillful general, she provided before the forces came into the field, for all the necessities of a victory, so that now the conflict was going on, she calmly surveyed its progress. It was noticed by the observing ones that the most of her time was spent helping to fill the baskets of certain shy, ragged boys, who had crept timidly into the busy circle.

Patience, seeing "Mose" and "Bill" hesitate at the door, invited them forward, and seated them in a quiet corner, where they could see but not be very generally seen.

"Mose!" whispered Bill, "them's nice looking folks tho' that's huskin' round that heap!"

"Yes, Bill, they be, but I feel dry a'ready. Don't you think John will have any liquor here on the sly?"

No, Mose. You'll need to turn into a pillar of salt and keep forever, if you think to sit here until John Alden does anything on the sly!"

One of the pleasant entertainments of the occasion, was a rivalry in filling the baskets with the husked ears. Clubs of three or more strove against each other for the palm. All, young and old, engaged in the exciting strife, and men full of years and honors, were for the time, young again, and joined in the happy shouts of the young over the victories.

"Mose, let's jine in that sport and beat them gals. 'Twould be something to brag on," said William Treat, becoming quite excited by the contest.

"I'm awful dry, I tell you, Bill. I think if John would bring on his cordial I might give 'em all a sweat;—shouldn't wonder in that case, if I beat the parson and the squire!"

Moses Pond went out to "wet up," and became too drunk to return. William Treat joined the husking circle, and soon felt John Alden's great, warm hand upon his head, and his greater, warmer heart beating in sympathy with his. It was the beginning of a new life, which gave promise of eternal life, to William Treat. On such seeming slender threads hang everlasting things!

The Crone boys, Ezekiel and Thomas, had had several trials with boys of their age. But somehow, the luck of Crone's Corner would follow them even to John Alden's husking. They were beaten every time, either because their unthrifty habits adhered to them, or because the presence of so many "great folks," abashed them to the disadvantage of their hands. Just as that expression — the great destroyer of true moral courage — "I don't care, — I won't try any more" — was about to seal their failure, Jane Curtis drew her stool in between Ezekiel and Thomas Crone, much to the disgust of the small aristocracy, and the delight of the true nobility such as John and Patience Alden. Miss Priscilla Codlin sneered at the act. "Do see," she whispered to a companion of like airs. "If there an't our minister's daughter gone to join in a trial with the dirty Crone children! I wouldn't be seen doing so if I was she!" Miss Codlin's grandfather was "a tithing man," and her father was captain of the town militia. The family was rising, so she stood on her dignity.

"Now, boys," said Miss Jane, "*we* will try. Come, Martha Turner, you get two more, and husk against us three. See you get two real smart ones or you will have no chance at all."

Martha was Deacon Turner's daughter — one of the nobility of the town — in unpretending intelligence and goodness. Martha sought two associates for the trial. She soon brought along a little hunchback girl, by the name of Martha Vose, but everybody called her Patty. Patty had a little body, but a great heart. Her hand was as tiny as a child's, and her voice squeaked and broke, in ordinary conversation even, like an invalid old woman's, though Patty was only twenty-two. But Patty Vose had a large brain, and she kept it well exercised in acquiring knowledge, and with thoughts of truth which pertained to this world, and that which is to come.

Martha next approached Miss Priscilla Codlin, daughter of Captain John Codlin. She was always very fastidious about being recognized as "the captain's daughter," seeming to think the "Captain" belonged to the family, and to herself in particular. The wits called her "Captain Priscilla."

"Come, Pris," said Mattie, in her innocent, hearty way, "You be one with me and Patty, to beat the Crone boys."

"Indeed, I won't!" exclaimed Pris, turning up her little nose — which was likely to be larger from its frequent exercise that way — and giving her head a toss. As to the tossing of the head, that was easy, there being so little in it.

"You won't, Pris! Well, then, I'll have—"

and Martha cast her eye over the busy huskers for a companion. "I'll have our minister's wife."

Away Martha went, crowding through the company, and stumbling over the baskets, now jostling this one, and then pitching against another, as full of merriment the while, as a child on Christmas eve.

She stated her case to Mrs. Curtis, and in her simplicity told who were the parties, and who had refused.

Mrs. Curtis saw how the case stood. Her husband, who stood by, looked a significant "go." These good people saw in this passing incident the workings of a true moral greatness in conflict with pretentious littleness.

So it turned out that the Rev. Mrs. Curtis, Martha Turner, and Patty, the pigmy hunchback, had a "set to" at husking with Jane Curtis and the two Crone boys, of Crone's Corner. Expectation stood on tiptoe. "Long time in even scales the victory hung." It was evident both parties were doing their best, and that there was to be no "giving in" to please somebody. Patty's little hands tore off the husks with evident exertion, if not pain, so, though she had the will, she counted but little in the contest. It was not *brain* work, or Patty would have counted a host.

"Tom," whispered Zeke, without abating a jot of his hot haste, "put in for dear life. The Crones will be somebody if we beat."

Tom did "put in." A new inspiration came over the usually crest-fallen boys. It might be a "silly" contest on the part of a cultured lady and the genteel young ladies, in the estimation of the Priscillas whose grandfathers were tithing men. But the *true nobility* said it was a sermon from the favored ones of the upper social circle, to the lowly and discouraged, on self-reliance. And the sermon bore fruit. The Crone side beat, and Zeke and Tom felt that they could look in the face every person at the husking. Though Priscillas may laugh at the assertion, a weight of no mean value had been thrown into the scale, which should lift the life of these burdened boys into a purer and higher sphere.

The husking had been going on from early in the afternoon. At an early hour in the evening John Alden's great "heap" of corn was in the corn house. The husks were pitched upon the scaffolding prepared for them. William Treat aided the latter work, much to the surprise of all except the Alden Farm folks. John had his eye upon just this class of people, and for them he constantly prayed, and for them, on every suitable occasion, he labored. More than in the yellow grain of his corn bins, he rejoiced in the God-given fruit of his moral sowing.

Zeke and Tom were now out of their corner and among folks. They volunteered to sweep up the barn floor, even hanging behind while other boys rushed to the new shed where the supper table was spread. John's eye was upon the Crone boys. He gave its true value to their every movement. He seemed to read their thoughts.

When all seemed to be ready, and the company stood about the well laden table, with keen appetites, not only whetted by long and earnest work, but by the enticing manner in which Aunt Patience had put her good things before them, the minister whispered to John, "Are you ready, brother Alden, to have the blessing asked?"

"Wait a minute, sir," said John, in an undertone, glancing along the whole line. He disappeared, while all stood waiting in solemn silence. He soon re-appeared with Zeke and Tom, pushed them in ahead of some of the boys who had come early to get the first grab at the food. He then nodded to the parson, and the blessing was asked.

Miss Priscilla's nose was turned up again when she saw this movement. George Hawes, who found capital for much fun in Priscilla's nose, said its condition was alarming, for it was certainly getting "out of joint." But William Treat declared that it was not alarming at all, for he was certain her nose had been "out of joint" with all her neighbors from the time her father was commissioned captain of the militia company."

William Treat ate a hearty supper without liquor. He looked round upon the happy company, not one of whom was drunk, and contrasted it with all other huskings he had ever seen. He put his hand upon his head. It did not ache as it had usually done on such occasions. He laid his hand solemnly upon his heart. It throbbed quietly, for he had peace within. Since he was a boy, he had not been home from any social or public gathering perfectly sober. He drew back from the gaze of the company and solemnly resolved,—"God being my helper, I will never touch the accursed thing again;" and the Holy Spirit in his heart whispered,— "I will be your helper."

The minister addressed the company a few moments. He said his time for retiring had come. Others might remain for social pleasure. He rejoiced in the happiness which beamed in every face, for all were sober. He thought his friends of Alden Farm were right, and that such occasions were better without strong drink. Pausing a little, he raised his voice and added with a clear, solemn tone, "I will go further, friends, and say that new light upon this subject rests upon my mind and heart. I believe that God will be honored and all the people benefited, if its use is wholly discontinued, except for a medicine."

The parson and the deacons retired. The young folks returned to the barn floor to play blind man's buff. Patty took her place on a stool in a little cuddy made for her in the hay mow by Mr. Alden. She shouted at the joy of others and none were happier than she!

The young folks, remembering that John Alden and Aunt Patience were looking on, gave the Crones a full share of the sport.

CHAPTER VIII.

AFTER THE HUSKING.

THE Alden Farm husking had cost its owner something. Patience and the children had worked hard to get ready the feast. The extra bill at the grocery was not small. The work of the next day in "righting up things," was considerable. Yet none concerned felt or thought that there had been any work. Love lightens burdens as to huskings as well as more important matters, and all had engaged in it with hearty good will.

"Now," shouted Carver, "hurrah for school! That heap of corn lay in our track! I guess we'll give the boys a sweat at school this winter. Do you know though we are to have a new teacher this winter, a real smart one they say, who knows as much as a minister, and not the old Granny we had last winter."

"Well, Carve," replied Miles, "I'm glad if our new master is smart, but you needn't call our good Master Paul a granny. It's kind of mean to kick a worn out horse because he don't draw as much as a young one. Father says that all he knows about ciphering he owes to Master Paul, and I'll bet father can cipher better than *some* young schoolmasters!"

Carver blushed at this deserved reproof, and like all manly, right-minded boys, took the correction kindly. "You're right, Miles!" he said mildly. "Master Paul *is* good, and knows lots."

The younger children had to run to the corn house to take a look at the great bin full of corn, and then to the barn floor to assure themselves that the "big heap" had gone. When they had fully assured their wondering minds of these important facts, which they knew well enough the night before, they all shouted "hurrah!" Jeremiah stood in the middle of the barn floor, and took his best position and put on his most important air, and exclaimed, "Look here, cows!" All the cows looked of course — twenty of them,— all having just eaten their breakfast, and so they had nothing else to do but look at Master Jerry, and listen. "Look a-here, cows, 'oo may have all 'em corn 'usks up there, and nobody else shan't have any!"

"Old Brindle" threw up her head, which was her way of saying "thank you!" and "Spot," a hearty young miss who didn't know when she had eaten enough, turned her eye up to the husks, as much as to say, "Give us some now, Master Jerry." But Jeremiah darted out of the barn, like a summer bird which had flown in to twitter for a moment, and then fly off to its mate in the tree top.

If the children of Alden Farm were happy so were the older folks. When John and Patience drew about the evening lamp, they talked over the incidents and results of the husking. Not a word was said of the work which had been done in transferring the corn from the barn floor to the corn house. That they appreciated, but there were other matters more on their minds.

"I do hope," said Patience, "that the Crone boys will fall in love with husking without liquor, and never get drunk again. Oh, if they could be taught courage to do right!"

"They went home with new resolutions to be somebody, or I cannot read human nature. But, Patience, did you see William Treat? yes, Treat remained to the last, drank the coffee and went home sober and with his wife?"

This was spoken with so unusual warmth for Mr. Alden, that his wife looked up calmly from her work, and remarked slowly and seriously, "How often are the resolutions of the drunkard like the early dew, soon gone! God grant that William may become a sober man. *He* only knows how much his family have suffered!"

"Didn't Parson Curtis speak out!" said John, starting from his chair with joyful excitement, and beginning to walk the room.

"I see," said Patience, smiling at her husband's warmth, "nothing but good to come of our minister's remarks. Let us thank God, John."

The great family Bible was taken from the stand earlier than usual. The children drew about their parents with fixed and loving eyes. It seemed to them that the precious Word never sounded so pleasantly from their father's lips. When they were all bowed in prayer, there was a sweet tenderness in the petition for the family of Ezekiel Crone, and for the complete and permanent reformation of William Treat.

"I mean to help Zeke Crone in his lessons this winter," whispered Carver to his brother, as they rose to their feet.

"I'll choose Tom on my side when we are playing," replied Miles, in a subdued voice.

Such was the spirit which prevailed at the Alden Farm after the husking. Let us look in upon some others who were there.

"Mr. Crone," said Jerusha Crone to her husband, as they drew up to their great back-log, which sent out its cheerful light and heat over the large kitchen. Ezekiel Crone looked at his wife lovingly and listened. He felt in a pleasant frame of mind, and there was a cheerful expression about the face of his wife, though tinged by a slight shade of sadness. "Mr. Crone, didn't John Alden have good luck as usual, to-night?"

"He certainly did," said Ezekiel. There was now a pause, and both looked into the fire. They neither knew why, but somehow both felt an embarrassment in speaking freely of the afternoon and evening. Zeke and Tom tarried unnecessarily long at the barn where they had been to put up the horse and to see if all was right. When they came into the long woodshed which opened into the kitchen, they lingered, but their cheerful chat, and occasional suppressed but hearty laugh were plainly heard, and declared their state of mind. The neighbor who had come to stay with the little ones, give them their supper and put them to bed, had returned home. When the boys reached the kitchen, their happy spirit still sparkled and run over, and for once, they met with no reproof for it. The family prayers were briefly offered, and soon after the whole family had retired, and the midnight stillness had stolen upon the sleeping household.

For many days there was with the parents an absorbing, and in some respects, a painful thinking. With Zeke and Tom there was an incessant happy talking. "Tom," said Zeke, as they trudged along to school on the Monday morning of its opening, "do you think we are to have a new teacher! A real smart one, they say, that's got more learning in his head than would split yourn and mine open!"

"Yes," replied Tom. "There will be one new scholar, too!"

"Who's that, Tom?" said Zeke, stopping and putting his hand on his brother's shoulder.

"It's this boy," replied Tom, straightening up as if able to look down upon his older brother. "Wan't we somebody at the husking, Zeke? didn't we help Jane Curtis beat the minister's wife, and didn't all the folks allow we were smart boys? I never knew it though, before, Zeke, for mother always said we were lazy louts, that never could be anybody; but John Alden told us just to do right, and hold our heads up with the very best."

"You're right, Tom," said Zeke, "only there's to be *two* new scholars. I believe that it's their father's and mother's talk at home, that's about all of it in making Carver and Miles Alden so smart at school. And," added Zeke, putting his mouth close to his brother's ear, and whispering, with deep emotion, "seems to me Crone's Corner has been more like Alden Farm since the husking."

Tom did not stop to reply, for he saw the Alden boys coming up the lane from their home, with their satchels in one hand, and each leading a sister with the other. When they saw the Crone boys they let go their sisters' hands and run, so that the boys went racing towards each other. Zeke and Tom *looked* the new scholars, as they walked with their Alden friends towards the school-house.

We will leave the boys for a while. It will take a little time—a few weeks at least, for those of each family to work out, and test by experiments their new formed resolutions,—the one to be helpers of the feeble, and the others to learn the hard lessons of self-reliance in doing right.

* * * * *

"How good it seems, William," said Huldah, the wife of William Treat, on the night in which they retired from the husking together—"How good it seems to have you come home with us, and"—Huldah stopped suddenly and looked her husband in the face, as if fearing to add "and not drunk as usual." The tear stood on her face as she missed the angry flash of a demoniac eye, and looked into, instead, the calm, affectionate countenance of her once loving, devoted husband.

"Say it, wife," he added — "not drunk! Fool that I have been! No rum at the husking to-night! No swearing nor fighting when it broke up! Huldah, didn't John Alden's lanterns light up the old barn gloriously! *Wa'n't* everybody brimming over with good feeling! Why, Huldah, John Alden's folks, and the parson's folks, and the deacon's folks, treated Bill Treat as if he was worth saving — and — Huldah — do you think," — and the penitent seeker of divine strength to lead a new life, buried his face in his hands and cried aloud.

"I think, my dear husband — I *know*, that by God's help, you can be a new man!"

After a few moments, in which a measure of composure came to both, Huldah took from a side table the family Bible. On the little stand, drawn towards the fire, she laid it, where, in other days, before the Rum Fiend had entered their family, it had been laid, morning and evening, and read at the hours of family devotion. "You did not mean, Huldah, for *me* to read and pray, to-night, wicked as I am!"

"Yes, dear," said Huldah, in a tone and with a countenance of tender entreaty. "What better can you do than to look into God's Word to learn the way back to him, and to pray to him to forgive and heal you?"

Whether by accident or design, William did not know, but when Huldah laid the Bible upon the stand it opened at the fifty-first Psalm. The prodigal read on with a melted and broken heart. When he came to the verse, "Hide thy face from my sins, and blot out all mine iniquities," he dropped his face upon the open Bible, and cried, sobbing, "Do, Lord!"

Huldah kneeled at the stand, reached up her hands and put them upon her husband's head and whispered the promises in his ear: "Though your sins be as scarlet, they shall be as wool, though they be red like crimson, they shall be white as snow." "Blessed be God who forgiveth our iniquities and healeth all our diseases." "But when the prodigal was yet a great way off, his father saw him, and had compassion, and ran, and fell on his neck and kissed him." The spirit of enduring, wifely, Christian affection, gave a wonderful sweetness to her utterance of these divine words, and the spirit of the forgiving Saviour gave them power to heal.

While the angels were rejoicing over the repentance of William Treat, there were those indulging towards the gathering in John Alden's barn, a very different feeling. Dr. Burt was not present, but when he heard what sentiments his pastor had there uttered, he hurried away to Deacon Prime's. The deacon was the senior official bearing that title. He was an old man, and was seldom now seen in the gatherings of God's people. He had been very jealous in his day, for the intregrity of the church over which he was set as an under-shepherd. His jealously had been mainly exhibited in hunting for heresy through the sermons, on the Sabbath, and for flaws in the government of their children on the part of the parents among the church members. He had studied theology under an old divine, six weeks, in his early manhood, aiming to be a preacher. This admirably qualified him to hunt heresy. He never had children of his own, which was an equally admirable qualification for him, and his amiable wife, to tell Christian parents how to bring up their households. To the good deacon Dr. Burt went with his heavy heart.

"Deacon," said the doctor, seating himself at a little stand on which the never failing mug of hard cider was sitting — "deacon, I feel our church is getting into a bad way!"

"I fear so too," said the deacon. "The doctrines an't preached as they used to be. The members are sadly remiss in correcting their children; 'Spare the rod and spoil the child,' is the text I've tried for forty years to impress upon the fathers and mothers of the parish. I've even offered, in some cases, to do the whipping of the youngsters for their parents, and they were ungrateful enough to tell me to mind my own business. I agree with you, doctor, that our church is in a bad way."

"Yes," said the doctor, solemnly, and our pastor has been to John Alden's husking, and —"

"There it is," interposed the deacon. "John's a good kind of a man, but he's been and got one of them ere stoves, and bricked up the fire-place of his father and grandsir! I do think it's wicked, doctor, to do so. Children should have more respect for them that's gone."

"I was saying," continued the doctor, "that our good minister—for I do believe he *means* to be good,— went to John Alden's husking, where John had set a table without liquor. John in so doing had reflected upon my professional judgment, which is, as is quite generally known, that liquor is one of God's good creatures, to be used lawfully. Now I hold that Mr. Curtis should not have countenanced him in so doing."

"You're right," said the deacon, taking up the mug of cider and drinking heartily.

"What's to become of the doctor's authority over young people in leading them into right habits concerning their health and morals, if farmers are to be encouraged in opposing them?"

"And what's to become of deacons too?" said the old gentleman, pushing the mug of cider towards the doctor, who nodded his thanks and drank lustily.

"But that's not all, deacon," continued the doctor, "nor the worst of it. Mr. Curtis made a speech, in which he commended John Alden's ultra notions, and declared that nobody ought to touch a bit of liquor of any kind who is not sick! and that's the gospel we are to have preached to us!"

"Dreadful!" said the deacon; "we must have a parish meeting called right off."

While the deacon and the doctor were maturing plans to stop the alarming developments of the temperance fanaticism of Alden Farm, Moses Pond came in. He came rather unceremoniously, having knocked and answered his own call most promptly. Mose was decidedly drunk,— that is, in the language of the conservatives, had been drinking "somewhat indiscreetly." "Sit down, Moses," said the deacon, "the doctor and I are considering important parish affairs."

"Yes," hiccoughed Mose, "and that's what I come for. Things are getting alarming down there to John Alden's house. Not that I believe in taking too much, though the best of us — yes, deacon — you know,— I say deacon the best of us will err sometimes, and be a little indiscreet.—"

"Be silent, Moses," interposed the doctor, "my professional duties require me to be in haste. I must finish without interruption, my business with the deacon."

This was spoken in a majesterial manner, and Mose subsided into quiet.

"I leave you, deacon, whose office it is, with your colleague, to direct in stopping this growing evil. Our good friend Alden, will, I trust, by proper church labor, be made to see the wrong of his well intended course, and —"

"There, now, doctor!" exclaimed Mose, rising and approaching him with extended hand, "I know'd you'n the deacon was on our side, and I told the tavern folks so —"

"*Sit down*, sir," shouted the doctor, bringing his foot down on the kitchen floor so violently, that the dishes rattled in the old cupboard in the corner.

"You're leetle hard, doctor, on your friends, what thinks as you do," muttered

Mose, sidling away to the cider, of which he took a large potation. "Deacon," he said patronizingly, patting him on the shoulder, and whispering in his ear, "your cider's the best in town. It's got the real grit to it! It's eeny most as good as the tavern rum."

The doctor left, and the deacon gave his attention to Moses. "It is plain," said the deacon, "that you have been taking too much. I'm agin that, as much as anybody. I say, Moses, to your face, that it is *wicked*." The last word was uttered with such emphasis, that it brought Moses to his feet.

"Now don't be too hard on a fellow that's on your side in the fight agin the Alden folks. I have — I confess it — I will, deacon — confess — I'm — I'm no hypocrite — I've taken a *leetle* too much, and I won't — no, deacon, I won't take too much, agin. I'll be very prudent. So, if you please, I'll take a drop of your cider, and be going.

There now, deacon, I pronouce that — yes — it's in my opinion the best cider in town — it's as good, any time, — yes, as good as the tavern rum. That, you know, — between you and I, — that's jest a leetle watered."

Moses Pond left, greatly to the relief of the deacon. The good man kept repeating to his wife, what, he said, he had always preached, both by precept and practice, that such drinkers as Moses Pond were wicked men, and their example was very bad. Every time the deacon repeated this, he said it with more emphasis. He felt that he must repel the sermon preached to him against his principles and practice on the temperance question, by the presence and agreement of Moses Pond. The ghost of his reproof would not down!

"Have you had a satisfactory call on the good deacon, Prime?" said Dr. Burt's wife to him, as he rather peevishly threw aside his coat and gloves.

Very," was the reply, "only Moses Pond came in, beastly drunk, to interrupt our consultation. Such fellows do annoy me greatly."

"Oh, pooh!" said his wife, "Moses is nobody."

CHAPTER IX.

THE NEW SCHOOLMASTER.

WINTER was reigning over New England. He had dropped his robe of white over fields and forests. He had frozen up the meadows, and made a solid foundation over which the farmer might drive his team. He had sealed over the pond, for the boys to skate and the girls to slide. He had spread his level covering over the brush and smaller obstacles in the woods, to the farmer's sled. The wood choppers were busy, in their frocks and heavy boots, loading the teams, before furious winds should pile up the snow and lay bare the ground. While the choppers scattered the chips with the vigorous blows of the axe, or thrashed their brawny hands, and stamped their feet, shouting joyously to the echoing woods, the wood-peckers answered with a busy, peck! peck! and the crow with an insolent, caw! caw! The squirrels for the most of the time, kept house, nibbling frugally at their winter store of fruit, and wondering what the use was of having snow to bury up the nuts. The rabbits left their clumsy tracks on the yielding snow, as they hopped from place to place, nipping at whatever the frosty winter had left eatable, listening the while with their great ears. The fox roused up in his den, and wondered at the din of men, birds and beasts, and said, in his foxy way, "When you are all still, and welcome night has come, I'll be round!" But none were happier than John Alden. The breeze which his raising and husking had stirred up in the parish, did not excite his resentment, nor annoy him. No drunken neighbor came to his house to claim affiliation with his principles or practice. No accusing ghost of conscience had to be talked down. John Alden's joyous feeling run over even, at times, and in one of these moods he declared to Patience that she had, during the last year, grown younger, smarter and handsomer than ever! Patience did not return the compliment, as her husband declared afterwards, he desired she should, but said in her quiet way, "John, you always was a boy, and you always will be a boy!"

We left the boys of Alden Farm and Crone's Corner going into school. Several weeks' experience has given them some acquaintance with the new master, and the kind of stuff their own good purposes were made of.

George Everett, the teacher, was a young man about twenty-one years of age. He was quiet and self-relying in school, never seeming disturbed, however suddenly any annoying conduct was sprung upon him, and never appearing at loss what to do in an emergency. His education was superior for his years and for those times, and to his scholars, his knowledge seemed immense. His calm, unyielding purpose in enforcing discipline, made him a terror to the insubordinate, and his sincere interest, expressed by self-sacrificing labor for the improvement of his scholars, made him the idol of those ambitious to learn.

Among the parents of the town, a difference of opinion prevailed in reference to the success of the young teacher. The friends of master Paul thought that it was a pity that venerable man had been set aside for an inexperienced stripling. Besides, Mr. Everett had brought with him some new notions about teaching, and had introduced some new text books. "Colburn's First Lessons in Arithmetic" came now into the school. Some laughed at it. "How many fingers have you got on one hand? How many on both?" "Pooh!" they said, "who couldn't tell that? We don't pay our money to a teacher to be spent in larnin' our children how many fingers they have got." Others, who dipped into it a little, said, "It's got no rules nor ciphering. Who ever heard of a 'Rithmetic without ciphering! It hasn't got no 'rule of three.'" It was as foolish as John Alden's stove, and as radical as his temperance notions.

The first evening that Carver and Miles brought home their "Colburn," they were full of glee about it.

"Carver," said Miles, "there is some hitch about this Arithmetic, I do believe."

"What makes you think so, Miles?"

"Why, when the master heard the boys at recess, laughing at it, he looked real funny; and when school was dismissed he heard Zeke Crone say he was going to go through it, and learn it all by heart, he laughed right out, and said that Ezekiel had not studied, he guessed, more than two pages of it."

"Well, Miles, here's a boy that means to examine Mr. Colburn's book, and see whether he knows as much about Arithmetic as your Ezekiel Crone, of that noted place, Crone's Corner."

"And here's a young man," said Miles, slipping his barn frock over his head,— "bother this frock," he suddenly exclaimed, pulling it back again, and fumbling about for the sleeve, forgetting at the same time the funny thing he was going to say in reply to his brother. "Bother this frock!" he again exclaimed, setting his milk pail down, and going to work more deliberately to see why the frock would not go on.

"You mean, Miles," said his mother, approaching him in her calm and quiet way, "that the frock 'bothers' you. There, my son, it's all right now. You had turned one sleeve inside out, when you took it off to put on your school frock. I suppose you was in the same hot haste then that you are now. Run now, or Carver will beat you in milking, and don't say 'bother it.' It may lead to a worse word."

"Thank you, mother," said Miles, catching up his milk pail and darting out of the kitchen door. He found his brother with one cow about half milked.

"I'll beat you to-night, Miles," said Carver.

"Bother — no, this old frock bothered me so," said Miles, a little vexed.

"Yes, and I saw you bother the frock this morning when you stripped it off in such a hurry to beat me in getting ready for school," said Carver, laughing.

Miles seated himself on his "milking-block," subsided into a calm frame of mind, and began to philosophize a little. "It's no use, I see, to be in such a hurry," he said, in a low tone, as if talking to the cow he was milking. "It only puts a fellow into a fret. I'll be as cool as my mother, and by"—he was about to say—"by jingo, I'll be as smart," but his mother's chiding about "idle words," checked him, and he simply but emphatically added—"I *wish* I could be as smart."

When the "chores" were all done, the supper eaten, and the family prayers, which immediately followed, were offered, Carver and Miles soon became absorbed in Colburn. The lesson was a long one, carrying the boys through the simple questions of the multiplication table, into the deeper mysteries of that wonderful little book.

"Mr. Colburn is somebody," whispered Miles, when he considered his lesson learned.

"His book isn't such *very* great things yet," said Carver, rather grandly, as he laid Colburn aside for "Murray's First Lessons" in grammar.

When the boys had returned from school, their father took up one of the Colburns.

He read quietly, on and on, looking for a while rather skeptical about this new way of learning Arithmetic. He was considered one of the best "cipherers" among his townsmen. He had mastered the "Rule of three," the second and last winter he ever attended school. "Reckoning" was his hobby, and in this he was almost equal to the minister, about as smart as the squire, and "the beat, any day," of the doctor. The more Mr. Alden studied the more he became interested. Weeks of the school term passed away, and the Alden boys had settled down into hard study over their Colburn.

"John," said Patience, one evening, laying down little Rachel's frock, on which she had been busily sewing, "what is there about that child's Arithmetic that interests you so? Are you getting ready to teach the 'ma'am's school' next summer?"

"Patience," said John, with one of his very quizzical looks, "let's hear you do this sum — right off now, in your mind, and no ciphering"— and then he gave out, "Six eights of ninety-six are how many sixths of twenty-four?"

"Pooh! John," said Patience, dryly, "that's nothing for anybody that's been studying it two weeks, every night except Saturday and Sunday night."

John acknowledged the justice of his wife's answer, and proceeded to enlighted her in the process of solving this puzzling question. Patience, who when a girl had "hated fractions," began to see a little daylight shining through them. Her husband was delighted with the interest manifested by his scholar. It became a new stimulus in his study, and he plunged deeper into the mysteries of the sensational book. At first he studied slyly, after the boys had laid the book aside. He now had them arrange their lessons the first hours of the long winter evenings, so that he might get his lesson.

"Carve," whispered Miles, one evening, "father ought to recite his lesson. Who knows whether he gets the answer to these crooked questions?"

"Maybe," said Carver, with a knowing look at his brother, "you'd better ask him to recite to *you*."

"Guess I'll study awhile first," replied Miles.

Two weeks more passed away, and Miles had become quite confident in his knowledge of Colburn.

"Father," he said one evening, in that playful manner which the children of Alden Farm learned of their parents, "*you* don't have to recite. I tell you, Master Everett puts us through!"

"Well," said his father, in an easy kind of way, "put *me* through, Miles,— only don't go *quite* through the book."

"Oh," said Miles, beginning already to back down, "we haven't been half way through yet!"

"He'll put *you* through before the play's over," whispered Carver. But Miles was not to be put down without a trial. He plied his father with questions which he had just conquered, with some promptings from his teacher. His father went through them to the children's astonishment, and the delight of Patience, who began to catch some of her husband's enthusiasm. The younger children listened wonderingly, and queried if *they* would ever know so much. Miles soon gave up trying to teach his father, and excused himself when asked by him to answer questions he did not know, by saying, "We haven't got to such questions yet."

But John Alden soon got beyond his depth. Yes, the little book, at which the boys had laughed, and the "knowing ones" had sneered, had defied, as he advanced, his patient thought and persistent puzzling. It was in vain that he scratched his head, tipped back in his great arm-chair, gazed at the ceiling, as if there was some wonderful thing up there, and *thought*. John Alden was a great thinker, but Colburn had drowned his deepest thoughts, even in his First Lessons.

Carver and Miles enjoyed their father's perplexity. It was fun to them, because he was always running over with good nature in such perplexities. They enjoyed it too, because their father generally found a way out of such corners, after a while.

"It seems to me, John," said his wife one evening, when he had spent much time puzzling over Colburn, "that a good deal of precious time goes with that Arithmetic. You haven't read much of any to me this winter, in Watts on the Mind, nor more than half through The Pilgrim's Progress. You have read them both through every winter before, since we have been married."

John took the reproof kindly, went to the book case, took down Watt's on the Mind, and read aloud for a full hour. For a whole week his wife did not see the little school book in his hand. Yet the puzzling questions were in his head, and he was continually seeking their solution. One Saturday he had an errand in town, but was gone much longer than usual. He had called at his friend's, Squire True's, where the schoolmaster boarded. Whether he had any special business at the squire's we do not know, but we are sure it was very gratifying to Mr. Alden to make the acquaintance of the new schoolmaster, and that it was easy for him to get into a talk about the new lesson book. The teacher was surprised to find in the farmer so much appreciation of the much talked of innovation in his method of presenting Arithmetic, and still more surprised when he learned that he had solved correctly most of its questions. By a little prompting, John's difficulties vanished, and he returned home, like a captain who had taken great spoils. That evening, a little while after the evening study hours had commenced, he took up Colburn for a short time, then slapped it together, laid it upon the stand and walked the floor with an air of triumph!

"Father's conquered Colburn," said Carver to his brother, in a low tone.

"Yes, every bit of it," replied Miles, without taking his eyes from his book.

The two boys felt as soldiers feel when they see their commanding officer rushing into the thickest of the fight. They were inspired to follow. Many were their stumblings, and many times they were sore vexed. But "I can't," "It's no use trying," "I mean to ask father if I may give it up and study something else," were expressions which never escaped their lips. To be sure they did get a little vexed sometimes, and their heads ached with trying. But their father's long puzzling, his patient, perplexed, but good-natured trying, and his final air of triumph, were to them like battles just won by their comrades to soldiers now fighting. There was victory in every sound, and success was breathed from the very atmosphere which surrounded them. John Alden had been lucky again, and his boys were declared by all the boys, "the lucky fellows who always come out ahead."

CHAPTER X.

A BREEZE AT CRONE'S CORNER.

"I do think, Jerusha," said Ezekiel Crone, "that our boys are getting along nicely at school this winter. I hope they'll have good luck until it closes."

"Yes," replied Mrs. Crone, "remarkably *for them*, and I do think, and always shall, though I suppose you'll give one of your provoking smiles when I say it, that it was my perseverance in teaching them the Catechism that gave them a good start."

"The husking at John Alden's," timidly suggested Mr. Crone.

"There it is," replied his wife. "You are so afraid that I shall have a little credit. Alden's folks must always be dragged in.

But if anything goes wrong with the children you are ready enough with your blame! Then it's, 'Jerusha, you was too hasty!' or, 'Jerusha, you needn't have spoken so!' but I'm determined the boys *shall* get along in school. If they don't, they mustn't think *I'm* going to put up with it."

Mr. Crone sighed when his wife began this strain, like a man who had just heard bad news concerning an absent friend. He soon after looked very thoughtful and anxious. But he soon began to drum with his fingers on the table. He then had resort to his ever present score book, in which he soon seemed absorbed.

Silence reigned awhile in the kitchen of Ezekiel Crone. The children were all in bed. The fire was burning low on the hearth, while the smouldering back-log occasionally sent out a flickering flame. The old clock in the corner seemed to tick louder than common, as if to warn its master and mistress of the lateness of the hour. The cat curled up in the end of the settle, sent out her low, dreamy purr.

"*I'm* going to bed, Ezekiel Crone," said Jerusha, suddenly starting up, and seizing a candle. "You may set and poke over that old score book as long as you please."

The Crone boys, Zeke and Tom, were astir early the next morning. They had planned to get a little time in the kitchen for study before the rest of the family were up. They were creeping softly down stairs by the door of the sleeping room of their parents. But their mother's ear was like that of a watch-dog, always open. She bounded from the bed, and opened the door. "What mischief are you up to now, you young rogues?" she exclaimed. "Where are you going this time of night?"

"We are going down into the kitchen to study," stammered Zeke. "The master says the Crones can learn as much as anybody, if they will. And we are going to try."

"Going down to study!" replied Mrs. Crone, with a sneer, which she could express like a practiced stage player. "Going to study!" she repeated with a withering look of incredulity. "Your father might believe such stories, but you can't cheat *me*. My closets have been turned upside down too many times by having you round before I'm up. Besides, you'll be setting the house on fire. No, go back to bed this minute, and don't you stir till your father calls you. *Then* do you get up instantly."

The old clock just at this moment struck four. Five o'clock was the customary hour of winter rising at the Crones'. The boys went back, put off their clothes, re-adjusted their bed, and lay down. For a moment or two no word was spoken. Strong emotions of anger and grief were struggling in their hearts for mastery, and as usual, anger soon held sway.

"It's no use, I'm not agoing to try to study," muttered Zeke, breaking the silence.

"Nor I either," replied Tom. "It's always the way in this house. If we are going to try to do anything right, nobody will believe us, and we are accused of lying and planning mischief."

There was silence for a while, when Tom said, pensively, "Zeke, them Alden boys have been real kind this term."

"Yes," replied Zeke.

Silence followed this remark, and the thoughts of the boys troubled them. The Alden boys had indeed been good friends, prompting them when necessary in their lessons, seeking their company in play, defending them against those annoyances which low minds delight to inflict upon the weak and the obscure, and especially, speaking those kind words of encouragement, which are often better to the halting, than great riches. They had promised to call at Crone's on their way to school, on the morning of which we are speaking. It was a full half mile out of their way. The Crones, delighted with the attention promised, had agreed to be ready in good season, and Zeke had added, "With good lessons all learned."

But their case was that of the soldier who fights after his army is defeated. Every sight and sound is depressing. The air is tainted with failure.

"Hurrah, boys!" shouted the Aldens, rushing into the great kitchen of the Crones, carrying an influence like the sudden overflow of a spring freshet upon a frozen meadow, driving the frost before it, and leaving springing grass and flowers behind it. "All ready, boys?" inquired Carver, in a quick, stirring tone.

"Most, wait a minute, Carver," replied Zeke, almost ready to burst into tears. "Got those splendid lessons you promised?" said Miles, and without waiting for an answer, rattled on — "Carve and I shot ahead this morning with our lessons like a rocket. We got up real early, and got more than an hour before chore time. We planned to steal a march on mother, so we got the wood and kindlings all ready the night before hand. We awoke about four o'clock, and crept down stairs as softly as mice, but I thought I heard mother laugh as we passed the door of her room, just as she does when she thinks she has got ahead of us. When we reached the kitchen, I'll bet there was a jolly fire! Mother had been down, made the fire, and gone back to bed again."

"That's just like mother," interposed Carver, "she was afraid we would lose a few minutes in getting the room warm."

Zeke and Tom were ready before this unwelcome talk was done, and their mother had hurried them off, hoping that Miles would cut his story short; but he lingered behind to finish it, and then followed the other boys like a race horse.

"Them Alden boys is real kind," said little Betsey Crone, looking innocently into her mother's face; "and their mother," she continued, "is real kind too."

"Your mother an't, I suppose!" said Mrs. Crone, sharply; "she never does anything for her children!"

The child slunk timidly away unable to see how she had offended, though she *felt* her mother's harsh rebuff.

Zeke and Tom did not respond cheerfully to the out-gushing good feeling of their generous young friends. Their very steps, as they loitered behind, seemed to say, It's no use; *we* can't, and that's the whole of it.

Carver, seeing this depression, so evidently different from the spirit with which they had parted the evening before, lingered behind, drew Zeke out and learned the history of the morning. Zeke could not refrain from tears, and, while he was telling his story, Carver wiped his eyes with the back of his hand.

Zeke and Tom Crone were detained at the close of the school in the afternoon of that day. All the other scholars had been dismissed. Their lessons had gone badly, and it seemed to the kind yet firm young teacher, that there had been no effort on their part to do better. He was a good deal puzzled and some vexed. He had spoken many kind, encouraging words to them, and given special assistance. His hope of their improvement had been raised, but the history of to-day had nearly destroyed it.

"It seems to me, boys," he said, in a tone of mingled grief and anger, "that you are bent on stupidity and idleness."

Just then a boy who had been crouching down under the window outside, in malicious curiosity, to learn the punishment which the master inflicted upon the delinquents, shouted out, as he ran away,—

"The boys of Crone's Corner,
Will be drones forever."

"I fear so," said the teacher, indorsing the bitter fling from the outside. Zeke involuntarily clinched his fist and scuffed his heavy boots on the floor. Mr. Everett understood this as a defiance of his authority, and an expressed contempt of his kind entreaties. He took a rattan from his desk, coiled at one end, and flexible at the other, being well suited to inflict stinging pain, without breaking the flesh or bones. He seized Zeke by the collar, and, with a sudden and violent jerk, laid him, with his face down, across the top of the desk. Tom started up, tossed his books into the middle of the floor, straightened himself up to his full height, and looked at the humiliating position of his brother, with lips quivering with excitement, and a face flushed with uncontrolled anger, bitterness and grief. The first blow of the rattan would be the signal for him to fly, reckless of consequences, to the rescue of his brother.

Just at this moment the door opened and Carver Alden rushed into the room.

"Don't strike him, sir! please, Mr. Everett, don't strike Zeke! He isn't to blame, nor Tom, neither."

The teacher paused. His first impulse was to strike Carver to the floor for his impertinent interference. But the boy's tender, beseeching face, down which the big, manly tears were rapidly chasing each other, and, most of all the profound respect and warm affection which he felt for the interferer, caused him to let go of Zeke and drop the rattan upon the floor. Zeke and Tom settled back into their seats. Their anger was gone at the first sight of Carver, and both buried their faces in their hands and wept bitterly. Carver laid his hand on the teacher's shoulder, looked up into his now placid face and whispered, "Please, sir, let the boys go, and I will explain all."

The tears of the Crone boys came to the

aid of their advocate, and the teacher said, with a faltering voice, and a bewildered look, "Go, boys."

Carver remained alone with the teacher. His self-imposed task was a delicate one. His sense of justice due to his young friends, whose case he was sure was not understood, and the explanation due to the teacher, compelled him to speak. But he was reluctant to criminate older persons than himself, and those who were the parents too, of his friends. What business was their management of their children to him? expressed a thought which troubled him. Then, he was not sure his parents would approve of his course. Under these oppressing and conflicting emotions, he was for a few moments silent. He saw in his teacher's gathering frown at his silence, a demand for an explanation. Carver instantly became calm under a sense of duty. He told simply and truthfully the incidents of the preceding evening, his promise to call for the Crones, their expressed ambition to be ready with good lessons, and then stated, delicately, Zeke's account of what had occurred at home in the morning.

The story of Carver fell upon the teacher like a revelation. It was, to his penetrating mind, a key which unlocked the secret concerning the Crone boys' character, which had so perplexed him. "It explains all!" he exclaimed, grasping Carver's hand cordially. "My noble boy!" he continued, "you have saved me from wronging the oppressed and doing what I never should have forgiven myself for, after learning what you have told me. Go, and God bless you."

Carver bounded towards the door. "Tell nobody of this affair but your parents!" said Mr. Everett, as the boy passed out.

"No, sir," just reached his ear, and he stepped to the window and caught a glimpse of Carver as he disappeared in the now gathering twilight, running with most surprising fleetness.

The Crone boys walked slowly homeward. The thought that "everybody is against us," would have been the burden of their minds but for Carver's timely interference in their behalf. They felt also that he was even then making a generous plea in their behalf. But discouragement weighed heavily upon them, and they sauntered homeward with a snail's pace. It was dark when they reached the kitchen, where they expected no word to comfort or inspire them. The barn chores were behind; the wood box was empty; the preparations for supper were not half completed, though the time had fully come; and the younger children were impatient and fretful.

"Well, you lazy fellows!" exclaimed Mrs. Crone, in an excited, harsh tone, "you've arrived at last. I suppose you'll claim you stopped to study, and try to cheat me at both ends of the day. I've heard how you have blundered through the day, and so had to stop and settle with your teacher. I hope he's flogged you both well."

Zeke was about to defend himself as he walked up to his mother with what little resolution the disasters of the day had left him. But Mrs. Crone seemed to anticipate the ground of his defense, and she prevented the utterance of a word of excuse, by exclaiming, in a boisterous tone, "There, be still! none of your sniveling excuses; you've had time enough, you know you have. I've done my best, mercy knows, to make something of you. Do you go, Zeke, and help your father in the barn; and do you, Tom, bring in some wood, and then help me set the table. There's nobody in this house to do a thing without I make a fuss about it."

Zeke's temper, which had not recovered from the strain imposed upon it at the school room, was not just now very amiable.

He muttered inaudibly as he was leaving his mother's presence. This was peculiarly unfortunate, as the mother's irritability was intense. Springing towards him, she gave him a rousing box on the ear. Zeke turned round and shouted spitefully, "Let me alone! Everybody blames or beats me. I wish I was dead!"

The unusual earnestness with which this was said, and the sudden uproar of the younger children, who began to cry violently, brought Mrs. Crone to a sudden pause. Zeke hurried away sobbing to the barn. In the meantime his mother hushed up the children, prepared the supper, and the whole family were soon gathered about the table. The countenance of every member looked as if they had suddenly been smitten by a pestilence. There was plenty of food, and it was served up in no mean style. Mrs. Crone's table cloth was snowy white. Her bread was of the best quality, and her pies the delight of all visitors to her house. The supper this evening was equal to her best. But it was eaten by the children as a frightened horse eats his oats — hesitating and half choked.

When the girls, Jane and Betsey, had gone to bed, and the evening candles were ablaze on the stand, Zeke and Tom took their place mopingly in the chimney corner. Silence reigned for a while. Mrs. Crone suddenly started up, and exclaimed, "There, Mr. Crone, do you see how those two great lazy boys waste their time? To-day both of them were detained after school, because they played the dunce all day, and disgraced themselves and us. Besides, Zeke was impudent to me to-night. They want the rod, *that's* what they want, and if you don't give it to them both you won't do your duty!"

Mr. Crone compromised between the requirement of his wife and his own inclination, which was to let the boys do about as they pleased, and began to scold them. Mr. Crone *could* scold. He was, in this respect, the superior of his wife; but carrying heavier shot, he did not fire so often, nor move to the attack so quickly. This evening every one of his words were like barbed arrows. They tore their way through the tender sensibilities of the boys, as a Minnie rifle ball tears up the flesh. Zeke's face indicated at one moment a disposition to stand up and fight, and at another an inclination to sit down and cry. Suddenly, as if his whole soul was in the purpose he had formed, he strode out of the room. * * * *

The old clock had struck nine, and all the family but Mr. Crone had gone to bed. No Ezekiel had returned. Somehow the father felt that some serious injury had been done by his cutting words, and that the consequences would not be seemingly harmless, as at other times. He had never considered that *every* word which had "provoked to anger," leaving "discouragement," had done his child a wrong, and that the accumulated effects overflow at last in desolating desperation.

Ten o'clock, and no Ezekiel! Mr. Crone took the lantern, and went out to the barn. "Ezekiel! Ezekiel!" he shouted, in a subdued and tender tone. The cattle yawned and looked amazed that their quiet should be disturbed at such an hour. He looked into the wood-shed, the corn-barn, and returned to the kitchen, set down the light, and took his seat on the settle, and looked into the fire. "I was a fool," he mused, "to indulge in such harsh language. The boys are not so much to blame, after all. They have no encouragement in this house to try to be anybody. It's all their mother's fault! It wan't my way to scold them, but wife made such a clamor about whipping, that I was driven to scolding. I won't do it again for any woman!"

Eleven o'clock, and no Ezekiel! Mr. Crone took the lamp, and went to his sleeping-room. He found his wife tossing in bed, in feverish excitement. "Has Ezekiel come?" she inquired, in a sharp, quick tone.

"No!" was the equally sharp and quick reply.

"Well, Mr. Crone, you needn't be so cross about it. If you'd whipped the boys, as I advised you to do, and been done with it, they would have been asleep this very minute, and my life wouldn't have been plagued out of me, as I believe it will be."

"And they'd been a world better off if I hadn't heard to you, and taken my own way, and let them alone," retorted Mr. Crone.

"I didn't advise you to scold them so, and you know it," exclaimed Mrs. Crone. "But then you must blame me, of course, or you'd never live through any trouble."

Mrs. Crone burst into one of her violent fits of crying, and Mr. Crone returned, with the lighted candle, to the kitchen. As he stood a moment and listened upon the stairs, as he passed down, he heard the suppressed sighs of Tom, whose eyes had not closed in sleep. He sat down by the kitchen fire, put on a fresh stick or two, which blazed up cheerfully, but it was only a mockery of his feelings. He crept up to Tom's bed-room, and whispered, tenderly, "Thomas, do you know where your brother has gone?"

"No, sir," was the reply; and Tom buried his face in the bed-clothes, and sobbed violently.

Mr. Crone's feelings were almost insufferable, and he watched out the weary hours of the night by the kitchen fire.

With heavy hearts, the Crone family published among their neighbors the loss of their boy. None had seen or heard from him. As day after day passed, it became the common talk. There were no railroads or telegrams, to spread the alarm, nor to bring in other exciting topics to displace the unpleasant one concerning the missing boy. Tom grieved, as did the other children, but kindly refrained from speaking of Zeke's provocation for running away. Some blamed the boy. "He was a stubborn, willful fellow," said they, "and his departure is no loss to the town. We pity the parents, but hope Zeke will find the world rough enough to bring him to his bearings."

"I don't blame the poor fellow!" exclaimed another. "He's been abused from his childhood. I hope he'll find a good place, and peace, somewhere, for he never had any at home. I hope now the Crones will treat the children which remain decently."

While people thus flippantly talked, there was real anguish of heart at Crone's Corner. The parents there loved their children, notwithstanding their unwise treatment. The daily petulance had given way to deep-seated grief. They were not understood, and few approached them with Christian words suited to their peculiar case. They had sinned. *That* they knew and felt; and that was what people most remembered when thinking or speaking of them. But they sorrowed deeply for their sin. *That* was what most of the people did not know, nor appreciate, if it were told them. But One knew. To Him they unburdened their hearts. The family altar became a place of penitent confession and tender entreaty. Little Betsey nestled affectionately up to her mother at such times, and was lovingly caressed. Peace, sweet peace, the "*My* peace," of the Prince of Peace, came to the family circle, as never before. How strange that the night of their sorrow had brought the noon-day light of Him who came a Light into the world!

CHAPTER XI.

THE WINTER SCHOOL.

CARVER ALDEN was late in reaching home, the afternoon of his interference in behalf of Zeke. Such an occurrence was very unusual, and as he had not intimated, even to his brother, the occasion of his lingering behind, there was some uneasiness felt concerning him. Beside, there was extra work at the barn awaiting him. Where's Carver? had been more than once repeated when he came bounding into the kitchen.

"Will tell you all about being late home this evening, when the chores are done," he exclaimed to his mother, catching up the milk pail and hurrying to the barn.

"Very well," said his mother, quietly. She

had not asked for an explanation, but expected one. Her son knew one was needed, and did not wait to be asked. He did not hesitate to explain, because he knew his explanation would be listened to, and kindly and candidly considered.

"Carve, did you stop to take Zeke's flogging for him!" said Miles, when they were left alone in the barn. "Hold the lantern so I can see if your eyes are not red. Maybe though, you stayed to take a flogging on your own account, against the blunders you are agoing to make! Now, Carve, if you did, just have the whipping transferred to *my* account. I'll do the blundering, and you take the floggings! Now that's a good fellow!"

"No, I *won't!*" exclaimed Carver, bringing his foot down with emphasis. "If Mr. Everett settled for all *your* shortcomings on my back, he would use it up in a week! But, Miles, you needn't try to be funny. I tell you what, I *do* pity Zeke and Tom. I should not matter one flogging if they could have a fair chance to go ahead in school for a whole winter. You ought to have seen how desperate Zeke looked to-night!"

"Did Mr. Everett flog him though?" interposed Miles, with serious concern.

"No," said Carver, dropping the conversation and starting for the house.

"I'll bet I see through it all," said Miles to himself; "Carve stopped to beg Zeke off. The Crones did blunder awfully to-day; and they looked so kind of stupid and discouraged. I wonder if they ever mean to be anybody!"

Miles did not know the history of the morning at Crone's Corner, as related to Carver. His musings were therefore a little hard on those he had tried so much to encourage.

John and Patience Alden heard Carver's straight-forward explanation without a word of comment. Patience wiped her eyes once with one corner of her checked apron when Zeke's trials were related. When Carver had finished, his father simply said, "Very well, my son," and resumed his reading. The boy saw approval in his parents' faces, and he settled down to his evening studies with a will.

When the children were all in bed, John Alden said to his wife, musingly, "Patience, I think I must reason with sister Crone. Yes, I must *reprove* her! She'll have to answer for the ruin of the boys!"

"Perhaps," said Patience, "she is not rightly reported by the boy."

"That's a wise thought," said her husband. "S'pose they would not thank me for interfering. Things do go askew though, there at the Corner." A silence, of some moments followed this remark, which Patience broke by saying in a solemn, feeling tone, "Who hath made us to differ?"

When the news of Zeke's departure was fully confirmed, the sorrow at Alden Farm was scarcely less than at Crone's Corner.

"I'll bet they flogged Zeke for getting home late last night!" said Carver, with a flush of anger quite unusual with him. The thought that Zeke was flogged after all, was too much for his good temper.

"I'd like to"— he was about to say— "flog old Crone, and I'll bet I could do it." But his eye at the moment met that of his mother's, expressing a calm reproof at his heat, and he brought a smile upon her face by saying with a sly twinkle of roguery, "I'd like to — yes, convince Mr. and Mrs. Crone that my father and mother's way of managing bad boys is a great sight better than their's."

It was a week after Zeke left before Tom came to school. It had been a week of weeping at home, but of such kindly words, and loving quiet, as the place had never before known. The work had been done with wonderful promptness. The hours about the evening lamp had been productive, notwithstanding heaviness of heart, of more work of the fingers and improvement of mind than at former times. Affliction proved a better condition for both, than the excitement of ill tempers. So Tom showed a preparation for his recitations which surprised the whole school. The Alden boys were watchful for opportunities to soothe his spirits and stimulate his zeal. The evident special attention towards him of the teacher, excited no jealousy. The taunts of the scholars directed against Crone's Corner, had ceased, with the exception of those of one boy. His persistent bitterness against the Crones requires a passing notice, especially in view of its cause and results.

His name was Fred Organ. He lived three miles from the town, on an out-of-the-way farm. His mother was a cousin to Mrs.

Ezekiel Crone. But somehow, as will unaccountably occur at times, among relatives, there had existed for many years a most bitter feud between the Organs and the Crones. They had watched for each others' haltings. They exchanged no friendly family visits. If any of the members met, it was in the most cold and formal manner. The Organs were not professed Christians, and they made the Crones the occasion of many a pharisaical sneer at the church. Now that Zeke had gone, nobody seemed to know where, they were afforded what was to them a rich topic of discourse. "I told you so," said Mrs. Organ. "God always punishes such bad family government, and such cruelty to their children, as there have always been at the Crone's. For my part, I'm no member of the church, but I do try to have my children behave decently. As to Zeke, I'm glad he's gone. He never did have any peace, poor fellow, and I hope he'll fall into good hands. I shouldn't wonder though if he had gone to sea! If so, he will catch a rope's end pretty often I'll be bound, and it will be a long time, if ever, before the Crones will hear from him. But it's good enough for them."

The Crones heard of the reproaches which their relatives cast upon them. But their hearts were humbled. They could forgive now. They even made advances towards a restoration of fellowship, but it was scorned.

So it naturally occurred that Fred Organ stood out, among his school fellows, in his persecution of Thomas Crone.

The weeks passed on. The winter had assumed its sternest force. The cold was at times intense. Yet Tom was always at school, and in season. One morning, the children awoke, and peered as well as they could out of the frost covered windows, and saw the drifted snow higher than the tops of the fences. The storm had been in a merry mood. Here it filled a door yard, blocking up the door, with a towering heap which reached nearly to the eaves of the house. Then it swept a clean path, laying bare the frozen sods and graveled walks. Now it shut the cattle up in the barns, as much as to say, It will not be for your health to leave your stalls. Then it just shook a barn door, to let the inmates know it was round, and passed by with its freight of snow, as if to say, You, cattle and horses, you had better walk out and see what's agoing on. There's no snow in your way.

Mr. Everett, the teacher, looked out, and remarked, "A small number at school to-day! A few living near will be there, and two boys from a distance — those of Alden Farm. Well, I must make it pay them well to come." Mr. Everett was like a sensible preacher who said he tried to preach his best sermons to the stormy day hearers. He went to his trunk, took out some blocks, then novel articles to explain some of the rules in Arithmetic. He took down a choice map which hung against the room wall, rolled it up, and put it under his arm. He also took along a rare work detailing some of the incidents of the American revolution, which every family could not get access to, as all can now. Thus armed he waded through the snow to the school-house. The faithful fire-builder of that week—for the larger boys took turns in building the fire and sweeping the school-room—had made the fire early, and the school-room fire-place glowed with its blazing sticks, and slowly burning back-log. The two Alden boys were already there when the teacher arrived. Soon, Thomas Crone came stamping into the entry. His face was ruddy with the exertion of wading through the drifts, and facing the still blustering wind.

"Well done, Thomas!" exclaimed the teacher, greeting him at the door. The few scholars gathered round him, one pulling off his frozen mittens, another taking his snowy cap which had been pulled down over his ears, and a third brushing the snow from his frock. The teacher invited the boys— about a dozen of them—to take a bench and draw up round the fire, placing his chair, at the same time, in one corner so as to face them all. After the devotional exercises, which seemed to the boys, more solemn than usual, the teacher proposed, much to the satisfaction of his scholars, to have what he called an "explaining session." He commenced with some of the most difficult portions which had been gone over by the first class of Colburn. He encouraged familiar conversation concerning the questions. The eyes of the boys fairly snapped with delight. They looked at each other with knowing nods, as if to say, Don't you see that? It's as clear as a whistle!

The blocks came next. They were inclined

to laugh at them. They had seen the babies play with blocks, and they could not see any other use for them. But when those who had been blindly following the rule in "Daboll's Arithmetic," on the square and cube root, saw the teacher's arrangement of his prettily finished pieces of wood, they jumped from their old backless, hard seats, and gathered about the teacher in an unrestrained expression of pleasure.

Next came the reading of "Incidents of the Revolutionary War." First, Mr. Everett read, and then passed the book to the best reader among the boys. The story was freely discussed, and the teacher, at the same time, made suggestions to improve the manner of reading. So the book went round. The boys were getting a stimulus to their taste for historical reading, and were learning too some important facts concerning the struggle of our fathers in throwing off a foreign government. But most of all, they were getting a healthful inspiration to study, the mainspring of all good scholarship.

"Boys," said the teacher, taking out his watch, and looking at it with surprise, "it is one o'clock, and you have had no recess, and no intermission for dinner."

"Why, Mr. Everett," exclaimed several voices at once, "you *must* be mistaken! It don't seem ten o'clock."

A half hour was spent in eating their lunch, while the boys, at the same time discussed the experience of the day thus far.

"It was pretty tough, boys, wading the snow this morning," said Carver, "and,— whew! how it comes against the window!— it will be tougher, I reckon, going home."

"Yes," said Thomas Crone, "it *was* tough. But I'm glad I came."

"Wan't Mr. Everett splendid?" whispered Miles. "I'll bet I can beat father in Colburn now!"

"I'm going to be a soldier, when I grow

up, and fight the British!" said the youngest boy of the group, Willie True, whose home was within a few moments' walk of the school house.

The fine spirits of the boys grew more intense as the teacher piled on the wood, and the storm without sung more and more uproarously its warning to those away from their own snug homes.

"We will have a spelling match, and go home," said the teacher, endeavoring to scratch the frost upon the window-pane, to look out upon the tempestuous scene.

"It will be too soon to go!" exclaimed Miles.

"I guess not," said the teacher, as a heavy gust of wind shook the very foundation of the school-house.

The trial of spelling was an exciting feature in most of New England schools of a former generation. There were no girls present at this trial, so the interest was less exciting. It is reported, in the accounts of these merry but profitable contests, that the girls beat the boys, "out of sight in a pair of minutes." If so our present champions were saved the mortification of such humiliating defeat. It may have seemed strange to the teacher on this occasion, but it turned out that the little William True carried off the greenest laurels; while the representative present of the Crones of Crone's Corner, came in next in the race, and quite near the victor. Spelling was the weak point in the scholarship of the Aldens. When hard study was required, or close and clear thinking, they were the leaders. In matters of memory they faltered.

"Good on Willie True, Esq.!" exclaimed Miles, when the school was dismissed; "he's a smasher at spelling. I am glad the girls wan't here to beat him!"

"Hurrah for Crone's Corner, which has beat Alden Farm!" generously shouted Carver. "Guess Miles and I will have to study up on the speller. But a plague take it, I'd rather study two Colburns and a Daboll, with Murray's Grammar thrown it!"

The countenance of Thomas Crone, which had worn for weeks a sad cast, lighted up with a momentary flush of joy. But it settled down into its customary shade of despondency as he buttoned up his coat, tied his comforter about his neck, pulled his cap down over his ears, and thought how Zeke and he had waded together, at other times, through such drifting snow. He was just about to say, "Good bye, boys," and "here goes!" when his father appeared in the school yard. "I was afraid, my son," he said, approaching Tom with a smile, "that you would get stuck in the snow. It's awful deep, and the wind cuts like a knife. Your mother would have me come. I would have harnessed up, only old White Hoofs never could have got through these drifts."

He then took Tom's hand and turned a resolute face to the storm.

"Was that old Zeke Crone?" said Carver, in a quiet tone. "That's not the way he *used* to meet the boys!"

Mrs. Crone had gone herself to the barn, and finished the chores which her husband was at work upon when she suggested that he go to meet Tom. "My boy,"—she most always called him "my boy" now—"shall have nothing to do," she said, musingly, "but to eat his supper and set down to his lessons." Her table was spread in her best style. The fire in the huge old fire-place fairly roared defiance to the storm king outside, and smiled warmly to his patrons within. Jane put her spelling book under her arm, to be ready to show Tom what wonderful progress she had made during the day, and little Betsey stowed herself away under the table to "scare him," when he approached the fire. There were no chidings now for these childish airs. The mother having assured herself that everything was upon the table, or "at the fire warming," for the supper, went frequently to the window, to endeavor to peer through the wintry atmosphere to get a sight of Tom and his father. But twilight had set in, and night was hastening on, although, as she said, it seemed only the middle of the afternoon.

Soon a cheerful shout from Tom announced their coming. The mother and the sisters flew to the door. "It's a glorious old storm!" he shouted, stamping vigorously, and throwing off his hat. His mother unloosed his comforter, helped him off with his coat, uttering, at the same time, hearty words of welcome. But a tear at the same time fell from her face. There was but *one* boy, she remembered, to welcome home.

"I'll finish the chores," said Mr. Crone, "and soon be in to supper."

THE WINTER SCHOOL. 193

"And I will help you, father," said Tom. "I haven't taken off my boots."

"I wouldn't go, either of you, out into this storm again," said Mrs. Crone.

"Why," replied Mr. Crone, "I shouldn't sleep to-night if old Brindle wan't milked, and the young stock hadn't the rest of their supper pushed up to them."

"Nor I either," replied his wife, archly.

Ezekiel at once read the explanation in his wife's pleasant face. "It was kind in you, Jerusha," he said, as they all drew around the inviting table. "It *is* pleasanter to sit down here than to go into the barn through the storm."

The supper being finished, the usual family prayer was offered. When the father requested of Him to watch over their lost one, his voice trembled more than usual, and the suppressed sobs were heard from every kneeling member of the family; and when he added, "Give him repentance unto life, and forgive us all our parental errors towards him," there came from the mother a scarcely audible, but deeply felt "amen!"

Tom had related at the table, with great animation, his success in the spelling class. "Why, mother!" he exclaimed, exultingly, "I beat both the Alden boys!"

"And so, of course, you beat all the scholars who were present," said his mother, with evident satisfaction.

"No," replied Tom, frankly, "Willie True beat me!"

All laughed at this, and agreed it would do very well for Willie to beat Tom if he could beat all others.

Jane and Betsey had kissed father and mother and brother, and said their "good night," and their prayers, and were fast asleep. Tom lifted up his eyes from his lesson, in which he had been quite absorbed, and observed the pleasant light which the fire and the candles threw over the room, and the quiet and loving, though sad countenances of his parents.

"If Zeke were here, how we could study now!" he thought, and in the depth of his emotion, almost said aloud. But he sadly reflected that it was not so when his brother was at home, and the Spirit of God whispered in his heart that this separation and its consequent sorrow was a part of the "all things" which "work together for good" to the trusting heart. He turned again to his lessons with a freer spirit.

The school term was fast drawing to a close. The spring, as its inspiring breath toned down the chilly atmosphere of winter, called upon all the young men of those days to exchange the school-room for the barn, and books for the plough and the hoe. The committee were expected to visit the school, to show *their* learning, and incidentally to ascertain how much, or rather how little, the children and young people knew by comparison. Those scholars who were conscious of having well spent the winter's privileges, looked forward to their coming with pleasure. The drones were already planning to find an excuse for staying away. The recitations were becoming exciting, for they were reviews, and Mr. Everett was evidently drilling his little army for the inspection of the review officers. In these daily general examinations, Fred Organ, the relative and persecutor of Thomas Crone, was dropping down towards the foot of his class. His temper, never amiable, was becoming heated with shame and envy. Just at this point of his school trials, Thomas spelt a word which he had missed, and passed above him. This was not all. The hated Crone was becoming the respected boy and scholar, gradually advancing in all his classes, and gaining daily upon the confidence of his teacher and schoolmates. More than once, Mr. Everett had said to himself, "I'm glad

I did not flog Zeke — thanks to Carver." Fred saw and felt all this, and it was as a thorn in his flesh. He wanted to "spite" Tom some way, though if asked for the reason, he probably could have given none better than that given by children often for their acts, "because I *wanted* to." Fred wanted to spite Tom, so when Tom was running swiftly in play at recess around the corner of the school-house, Fred put out his foot and tripped him up. The fall was a heavy one, and as the boy struck the frozen ground, a serious gash was cut in his head, his hands were torn by his effort to break the fall, and his knees were badly bruised. He was taken up bleeding and groaning, and carried into the school-house, the object of the sympathy of all, while a cloud of angry countenances lowered over Fred.

"I didn't go to do it," whimpered Fred, beginning to be alarmed at what he had done.

"You did! You did it a-purpose. I saw you!" exclaimed Willie True.

"I wish the law *required* me to whip Fred; because I would discharge my duty so faithfully!" said Miles Alden, as the boys were rushing into the school room at the call of the bell.

"The law of God, Miles?" inquired Carver. "But it don't; now straighten out your fist, and don't go to acting the bully! Fred will catch something worse than your mosquito bites."

Miles nodded assent, as he blushed and fell back upon his mother's saying, "Hot tempers make bitter repentance."

The incident broke up the remaining hour of the session, and the children were dismissed early, carrying, as they scattered through the district, a fresh and eagerly improved topic of gossip. Thomas was carried home, and was found more frightened than seriously injured. The flesh wound in the head, and the bruises upon his hands and knees were soon healed by good care on the part of his mother. There was no blaming now the bad luck of Crone's Corner. The unusual sympathy on the part of the neighbors surprised the Crone family. The incident soon grew, in their estimation, into a cause of gratitude — a cloud tinged with a golden sunrising, — as it brought out a growing respect for them and their boy.

CHAPTER XII.

THE EXAMINATION.

EXAMINATION DAY came at last. Mr. Curtis, the minister, was there, the most deeply interested of all the committee, because the most appreciative of what had been done by the faithful teacher. Deacon Turner sat near to, and leaned upon the judgment of his pastor in matters of learning. Squire True was more independent, and was only a little jealous of any departure from the old paths. Dr. Burt looked through and over his spectacles with *awful* gravity. His wisdom was that of an owl in an ivy bush. Old Deacon Prime was there, in a seat of honor due his age and sacred office. He was not *of* the committee, but *with* them — that is, if they scolded the boys, solemnly lectured the girls, commended what was old, and scouted that which was new. He was called upon to make a prayer at the opening of the exercises, and he did so, under a solemn sense of the responsibility of giving thereby the true key-note to them. He remembered to implore pardon for the great waywardness of all children at the present time. He told God, with great emphasis, that Eli's sin was never so prevalent as now. He asked that the committee might have moral courage to do all their duty, and rise above a slavish and sinful fear of man; by which he was uncharitably understood to mean that the committee should condemn everybody in general, and all young people in particular, except the chosen few whom Deacon Prime represented, and with whom the wisdom of the town was expected to die.

The exercises commenced with reading. Some humorous pieces were read, in which

Mr. Everett had taken great pains to secure in his pupils, a natural expression, and a just modulation of the voice. Deacon Turner's daughter, Martha, and Miles Alden, entered into this kind of reading with spirit. It was a little in the line of their exhuberant love of fun. The teacher, with an excusable weakness, showed them off by giving them each a select piece, of this character, from his own library. For a moment or two the solemn gravity, for which such occasions had been noted both before and since the fathers had fallen asleep, was broken down. Mr. Curtis and Deacon Turner smiled, Squire True was not seen to scowl, and so the school and the greater part felt at full liberty to laugh, which they did, much to their satisfaction. John Alden sat, fortunately, in a corner, a little out of sight from Deacon Prime's seat, for he laughed until his face fairly glowed.

"This is truly awful trifling," whispered Deacon Prime to Doctor Burt.

"It is," said the doctor, "and something must be done about it."

Next came an examination in the innocent but mischief-making little book, "Colburn's First Lessons in Arithmetic."

"Tut! tut!" said Deacon Prime, reading the first few questions, "what have we here?"

This was said in an undertone to Dr. Burt, who replied, "It's one of the new teacher's follies. It's got no Rule of Three in it!"

Both looked very solemn during the examination, which was very spirited, giving earnest of the revolution in our schools in the method of teaching Arithmetic, which this text-book has effected. Mr. Curtis was delighted. Deacon Turner had given it a sufficient examination to see its great value. Squire True looked puzzled, and was disposed to keep his opinion of this part of the examination to himself. But John Alden held a copy of the book in his hand, and seemed entirely absorbed in the way the scholars answered the questions.

But we will turn our attention to a few of the scholars. There was the minister's daughter Jane, who showed not only her own diligence and good sense in her studies, but her parents' promptings in them. She was quiet, ready, and self-possessed. Martha Turner's eye meant fun all through the examination, though she was a deacon's daughter. But she did not discredit her father's sacred position in the church. She never made fun at the cost of a schoolmate's good name, or sensitive feelings. It was a pleasantry which lifted many a desponding one over a hard place. It was a sunbeam often to a darkened spirit. Her wit, which was keen, was always indulged in behalf of the weakest party in a dispute. She had been the uniform friend of the Crones, and when Zeke disappeared from the school, his home and the town, she wept like a child. She made the scholars slyly laugh when she looked at the sombre faces of Dr. Burt and

Deacon Prime. The doctor was positively vexed to meet the mischievous glance of her eye. He would have tried to trip her up in her recitations, but he felt that the experiment would be dangerous. Deacon Prime thought, when he looked at her, that it was plain that his Brother Turner did not make a sufficient use of the rod in his parental government; but the scholars, especially the little ones in the profound study of the Primer, thought that she was "just as good as she could be," and one little "Tot" declared, with great solemnity, that it was his opinion "Mattie Turner was one of God's angels run away from heaven to come to their school." What the larger boys thought they were not so free to say.

Carver and Miles Alden passed the examination like boys who had *studied* and *thought*, without having any ability to shine. They looked self-relying and happy. But the scholar towards whom all eyes were directed, was Thomas Crone. His head was still bandaged, which, with his lonely look without Zeke, excited sympathy. Then there was so evident a determination to struggle out of the low position in school which the Crones had occupied, and so much in his countenance which seemed to confess his present inferiority, that every right-minded looker-on wished him success. It was evident too, that the teacher was ready to give him every fair means of appearing well; indeed, it was plain that he slightly petted him. The spelling match was the last exercise before the committee. Nearly the whole school was arranged around the sides of the school-house, and across the front seats. It was an exciting time for children and the parents who were looking on. Even the Alden boys looked just a little anxious for the result. They had stood the fairest and most thorough test of good improvement in all their recitations thus far. The spelling book had been studied by them carefully, their mother, who knew their weakness in this study, having prompted them often by her sensible remarks of its importance. Still, somehow, spelling slips from some minds, as money does from a spendthrift's fingers. It seemed to do so at times from Miles and Carver. "Yet," said Miles, "we'll spike the words into our noddles, won't we, Carver?" And they had, by dint of hard study, "spiked them in." So they appeared in the hour of trial, before the august committee, with only a little perturbation,— just enough to aid rather than disturb their memories.

Martha Turner's face, as she stood in the class, waiting for the coming conflict, was wreathed in smiles. It seemed to say, "I will enjoy somebody's success, if not my own."

Thomas Crone never looked more intelligent and attractive. His usually dull countenance was animated. He stood erect, the conscious equal here, of the majority of the school.

Dr. Burt commenced the examination by giving out words of

"Learned length and thundering sound."

The class had learned that such words are not the hardest to spell. The words went round, and only one scholar sat down, he having just tripped a little, when the stern voice of the doctor growled, "Sit down, sir." He gave the Speller to Deacon Prime, who prefaced his part of the exercises by some grave remarks on the great neglect, now-a-days, of spelling, while so much time was given to "light reading," and trifling little books like the new "Rethmetic." He then gave out words, over which he first paused, spelling them out himself. Two more failed, and were sent, with a solemn admonition, to their seats. When he put the word to Mattic Turner, she paused, just a moment, as if hesitating about the spelling. But it was like the pause of a racer who feels sure of winning the race. She fixed, the while, her quizzical eyes on the deacon, until every scholar was ready to laugh outright. He *felt* the joke, and was provoked, but the shot that annoyed him was from a masked battery, and he dared not move. He was about to say "the next," when Mattie spelt the word so glibly, and with such force and distinctness, that every syllable shot through him. He passed his book to Squire True, and sat down, feeling like a man who has been thrown in a wrestling match.

The squire was coldly fair, gave the class a rather easy word round, and called upon Deacon Turner. The class at once relaxed from their stiff attitude, into an easy position, as in the presence of a friend. Sympathy is electrical. It is not seen but felt; nor can one always tell whence it comes or whither it goes; yet its presence can no more be mistaken than can the presence of sunshine. So the class were at once in the most cordial sympathy with their examiner. It was as if one of their own number asked the questions. The words given out were harder to spell than any before given, yet none missed.

Mr. Curtis was now expected to put words to the class, until all but one should have missed and *set* down, and he brought the trial to a speedy close, by giving them short words in common use, which sound alike, but have a different spelling and meaning.

Thomas Crone stood with the four last — the others were Martha Turner and the Aldens. The first cloud which had been seen on Mattie's face, lingered there for a moment when Thomas tripped and sat down. She declared afterwards, that if Tom had beat the Aldens, she would have spelt the next word wrong on purpose. But she tried her best to beat Carver and Miles, and she did it.

Now came the "remarks." It was already late. The little ones lolled wearily from side to side. Mr. Curtis spoke a few words of discriminating praise. He commended the labors of the teacher, "as faithful, thorough and progressive." Deacon Turner thanked God that he was permitted to see his children enjoy privileges so greatly in advance of those he had received. The squire said that all had done "very tolerably well."

"Be faithful, Brother Burt," whispered Deacon Prime. "My infirmities won't let me speak."

The doctor rose with great solemnity. It seemed to the children to grow suddenly darker in the school-room, when he stood erect. "I have," he remarked, "a duty to do, which I dare not evade, though it is painful to the flesh."

Deacon Prime nodded assent, and actually smiled.

"There has been great levity in the school-room to-day. And it pains me to be obliged to say that this was encouraged at the very commencement of our exercises, by your teacher, in the kind of reading lessons given to the scholars."

The doctor looked over his glasses, right at the young teacher. Deacon Prime groaned audibly. Mr. Everett had taken his chair at the commencement of the addresses, and, very accidently of course, placed it against the end of the seat in which Mattie Turner sat. When the doctor uttered his reproof to the teacher, she leaned forward before him, so that her eyes took the range of the doctor's, and screened in part those of her loved instructor's. The scholars, in turning in the direction of the speaker's withering gaze, caught Mattie's bewitching glance. To every boy and girl of them, her eyes exclaimed, right in the doctor's face, "Oh, fudge!" There was a twitter all over the house. The vanquished doctor sat down in confusion. Deacon Prime groaned again, louder than before. An old lady who sat near him, not quite comprehending the situation, but seeing the deacon clasp his hands together and roll up his eyes as if in pain, leaned forward and whispered, "Lor sakes, deacon, what's the matter? Are you sick?"

Mr. Curtis arose just at this moment. He said he was aware that the session had been a long one, and that it was now late. "But," he continued, "there is one warm friend to our children, who is deeply interested in their improvement. You will all be pleased to hear from him. Brother Alden will make some remarks."

The uneasy rustling at once ceased. The eyes of the little ones sparkled with delight at the sight of him, as he came forward from the corner in which but few had noticed him. The teacher came forward nearer to the speaker. Thomas Crone's sad countenance lighted up, as does that of a stranger when unexpectedly meeting an old friend. Dr. Burt tried to look indifferent concerning what a rough, uneducated farmer might say, but he could not forget, and he would not forgive, the humiliation inflicted upon him when he went to Alden Farm to teach its proprietor the true doctrine of temperance. So he tried not to care what he might say, but his restless eye, uneasy hands and nervous moving about, betrayed him.

"My friends," said Alden, speaking with honest directness and force, "I have experienced a loss by this school this winter." He paused, stood erect, and looked coolly at the dignified committee. The teacher and scholars seemed a little puzzled, but felt assured Mr. Alden would come out on their side. Deacon Prime hastily inferred he was coming out on the side of the croakers. He whispered, leaning forward and directing his remark to Alden, "You mean, Brother Alden, that your children have experienced a loss by the school."

"No *sir*," thundered Alden, with a look which wilted the deacon. "*I* have lost by the school! I have lost my prejudice against a young teacher, who has proved that his head is well informed, and his heart in the right place. I have lost my prejudice against new books for our children to study. The new Arithmetic has woke up my youngsters' faculty of reckoning amazingly. It has put thinking and study into them. We have had Arithmetic questions at Alden Farm for breakfast, dinner, and supper."

The scholars laughed, the teacher and minister smiled, Deacon Prime sighed, and the doctor scowled.

"I have lost still more," continued Alden. "I have lost the chopping of full a cord of wood! My boys were a little more interested in school than work, though they have worked with a will, and I have caught the study fever, and it has cost me, friends, the chopping of a whole cord of wood!"

John Alden screwed his mouth round into such a funny pucker when he said this, and looked at Deacon Prime with such a comical air, that the whole school laughed outright. The deacon rested his elbow upon his knee, his chin upon the palm of his hand, and sighed. He did not look up, but his ears took in the painful sounds of levity. Dr. Burt was not so meek. He held up his head and *looked* fight. He was just about to be rash enough to reprove the school and the offending speaker, when Mr. Alden proceeded. "But I have received in place of the labor of chopping a cord of wood, more knowledge of Arithmetic than I ever had before. My boys have had excited in them a thirst for study and learning, that I esteem of more value than my whole farm. It's my opinion that a new era has commenced in the history of our school, from which shall date greater progress by our children in useful knowledge than ever before. My losses, then, friends, have been great gain. I hope we shall go on losing and gaining in this way for years to come."

Thus closed the winter term of the school. The scholars gathered about their teacher uttering their "good bye" with a cordial and sincere interest. "I thank you, Mr. Everett, for being so kind to me," said Thomas Crone, timidly. "I shall *try* to be somebody!"

No farewell word fell on the teacher's ear more gratefully. It was the hopeful word of an oppressed heart struggling upward under the warming beams of his Christian kindness.

For weeks after the close of the school, every household of the town took up the subject of "our school." The evident improved interest of the children in all school studies silenced all disparagements. John Alden's speech was another hit of his good luck. His influence for good was never greater.

CHAPTER XIII.

PATTY VOSE.

AMONG those who were vexed at the altered spirit at Crone's Corner, and who found some way to account for it without allowing any improvement, were the Organs. "Crones will be Crones still," said Mrs. Organ. "It's all *outside* washing; they are the same old hard folks at home, I'll warrant."

But the evident improvement in Tom, and the different bearing of his parents towards him, which was apparent in so many ways, were opposed to her assumptions. But this only made her the more clamorous. She was provoked too that her Fred had fallen behind Tom in his classes, and was generally very much blamed for his bruised head, though she stoutly contended that Tom's fall was an accident. It began to be noticed that the more sympathy the people of the parish manifested for the Crone's, the more bitter and loud were the Organs in decrying them. If Zeke was named, and pity was expressed for his parents, Mrs. Organ grew red in the face with excitement. Her words of denunciation at such times, of their treatment of the missing boy, whom she called "poor fellow," knew no bounds.

Among those who greatly rejoiced at the hopeful look at the Corner, and the history during the winter, of the school, was Martha Vose — known as Patty, — whom we met at the Alden Farm husking. Her dwarfed body and shriveled limbs grew neither stronger nor larger. But her mind had caught fresh vigor from the labors of the young teacher. He had visited her often, and through his occasional help she had thoroughly learned Colburn's Arithmetic. It would not have done for the croakers against the school to come within Patty's reach. Gifted with a fine flow of language, perfect self-command, and a Christian spirit which grew daily more Christ-like, she disarmed her opponents of all prejudice against what she had to say, and then stated and urged her case with melting power. Thomas Crone had just begun to find in her an ever ready helper of all his manly efforts of self-elevation. Patty's home was an humble, but comfortable one. She was the only child of a widowed mother, who owned the house. A barn, a garden, a small orchard, and a few acres of land, belonged to the place. These last the widow Vose had sometimes let, or otherwise turned to profit as best she could. Patty took in sewing for the neighbors, and her mother was an ever ready helper of the sick of wealthier families, by which a comfortable income was secured. So the two lived for and in each other, in frugal independence, owing no man and envying none. Charitable offerings did not often enter, but frequently went from their home. But above these they had a priceless treasure to bestow which made many rich. They bestowed, by example in holy living, by a Christian spirit which breathed in their words and acts, and by a divinely inspired wisdom which distilled as the dew, treasures of grace. Those seeking to know Christ found in them apt teachers. The burdened in heart often went away casting all their care on the great Helper. The desponding were cheered, as much by the atmosphere they breathed at "Hope Cottage," as by the words which were spoken. All classes of people, who loved the atmosphere of a Christian home sought Hope Cottage. Gossipers avoided it, for it became well understood that for them no listening ears were there. Mere idlers did not go, for Patty was always busy except when there was good to be done.

"Patience," said John Alden to his wife, soon after the school had closed, "what a spirit of study does possess our boys! I overheard Carver and Miles, as they were shelling corn this forenoon, talking over their plans; Miles said he was a-going to be a great statesman, for Mr. Everett said a boy could make himself, by hard work and an honest heart, about what he pleased. Carver said he hadn't made up his mind what he should be, but, 'maybe a minister.' They seemed very serious in their talk, and hinted at plans for study during the summer. Now, Patience, I kind of hate to keep them to work all summer on the farm. Maybe their relish for books will die out over the planting, hoeing, haying and harvesting."

"I've been thinking of that myself," said Patience, in her peculiarly quiet, thoughtful way. "I have a plan in my mind," she added, without emotion, and without taking her eyes from her work.

"There, Patience!" exclaimed John, with animation, "you are always getting ahead of me by your plans. Let me tell you *mine* first."

John moved his chair up nearer to Patience, and looked lovingly into her face, and remarked, roguishly, before detailing his plan, "A man don't want always to be indebted to his wife for the best management. It's been the plague of my married life!"

"You're a boy, John," said Patience, turn-her face dangerously near to his, and adding, "Now do state your plan."

"You know there is old Dr. Peters' Academy on Cedar Hill. It is not more than twenty miles from here. He is said to be a good scholar, only rather stiff and formal. After the spring planting is done, we might spare them until fall. I won't turn up so much ground as common, and we must economize, for the sake of educating the boys. Who knows, Patience, but God may convert

Carver and Miles, and make one a minister and put the other into a place to bless the country? You can fix up their clothes as no other woman can, and they won't be extravagant, I know."

Mr. Alden was disappointed, and almost vexed — would have been if grace had not long since taught him a better way — at Patience's cool and simple nod of the head, at each point in the development of his plan. He waited awhile for an enthusiastic concurrence, but none being tendered, he tipped back in his chair, clasped his hands behind his head, and asked, "What do you think of my plan, Patience?"

"Rather expensive," remarked Patience, working with renewed diligence.

"We have a few hundreds laid up, you know?" suggested her husband.

"But you'll want that when they go to college, maybe."

"College!" exclaimed Mr. Alden, starting

to his feet and pushing his fingers through his hair, and brushing it up until it stood erect on his head. He began to understand Patience. She was taking a more comprehensive view of the boys' education, than he had done. "But," he queried, "they must go to the academy before they go to college?"

"Now, husband," replied Patience, laying down her work, and turning towards the fire, and pointing to a chair to have him sit down by her, "there is where I think your plan is faulty."

"What do you propose, Patience?" said Mr. Alden, drawing his chair close to that of his wife.

"Why, send them to Patty," said Patience, decidedly.

John was silent for a few moments. He then began in his usual thorough way to turn his wife's plan over, and look at it from every point of view. The more he did so, asking questions and suggesting objections, the more he liked it. Patty had studied Latin and Greek under Mr. Curtis' instruction, for several years. Mr. Curtis had prepared several young men for college, was known as a thorough scholar, but was too much engaged now in parish matters to do so. He had often said that Patty was more critical in the languages than most of his college classmates. She was an enthusiast in these advanced studies, reading them as most of her age read the lighter literature.

"Old Dr. Peters of Cedar Hill Academy," suggested Patience, "is about like, in his sphere, our old master Paul, who taught our school so long. He don't love boys. I don't believe in a teacher who don't love boys."

"You are right," said John. "Our Miles said when the doctor preached for Mr. Curtis, that his face looked as if it were bitten some time by a January frost, and never thawed out."

"The boys are at that age when their moral improvement is best given at home."

"Right again," said John, growing warm in his admiration for his wife's plan.

"If they remain at home," continued Mrs. Alden, "they will be under the preaching and pastoral care of Mr. Curtis, who says he sees some signs of the outpouring of the Holy Spirit upon us. If that comes, we shall want the boys here, you know, to share in its great benefits."

Mr. Alden assented with increasing emotion, while his wife quietly added, "They will be at home, too, to assist you night and morning, and to come to your help in any emergency on the farm. I have a notion that some out-door work does not hurt boys who study."

"There it is again!" exclaimed Mr. Alden, "my plan is all upset by a woman! It's nowhere when compared with my wife's. You *are* a witch, and I'll have you reported —"

"Don't, John, they hang witches!" interposed Patience.

"I will, though! This very week I'll report you — to Patty, who shall know how you bewitch me out of my own plans into an adoption unanimously of yours, and she shall render a verdict in the case."

"Patty is mercifully inclined," remarked Patience.

Patty was delighted with the proposal from the Aldens. Arrangements were at once made in reference to the hours of recitation each day. The boys were to continue their English studies, giving them at present the most of their time, with easy, occasional lessons in the Latin Grammar. They were to do all the work, in return, on the little farm of Patty's mother. Besides, there was to be such money payment as might seem right when the plan was in full operation. Patty knew she was safe in leaving the final compensation to Mr. Alden's judgment and sense of right.

Carver and Miles were jubilant when the arrangement was announced to them. They lay awake full two hours that night, after they were in bed, maturing the spring and summer campaign.

"Won't we," said Miles, "make the widow Vose's old place shine? It won't take much of our time, neither."

"And father shall see that we can help him too," chimed in Carver. Thus devising "liberal things," the boys fell asleep.

Gossip was soon astir to discuss the new move at Alden Farm. Old ladies looked over the tops of their spectacles and exclaimed, "Lor sakes! what won't John Alden do next!"

"What are we coming to!" exclaimed Deacon Prime; "women teaching big boys! John Alden had better keep his boys at work, and not spoil them with high notions about larnin'."

But Mr. Curtis was decidedly gratified

with the arrangement. "It will be for the benefit of all the parties concerned. The boys will be well instructed in their studies, and favorably impressed with regard to religious things. Brother Alden always looks carefully into matters before he moves."

But none were more impressed with the importance of this enterprise, than Patty herself. She commenced immediately a careful review of her studies, while at the same time she was much more engaged in reading the Scriptures and in prayer. She seemed lifted into another sphere, intellectually and morally. It appeared to her that she now understood why God had given her from a child, a great thirst for knowledge, and unusual aptness in attaining it. She thankfully, too, acknowledged His hand in opening to her a long desired path of greater usefulness. Her deformity of body had been, in earlier years, a source of deep grief to her. She often went to bed in tears and bitterness of spirit, after seeing a company of rollicking children. Now she thanked God for *all* His dealings with her. She felt that while he had withheld with one hand, he had bountifully given with the other. "The peace that passeth understanding," filled her heart, and thanksgiving and supplication were constantly flowing from it to the Great Giver.

None who knew Patty's frame of mind were surprised at a new feature which she proposed in reference to her anticipated work. She came from her sleeping room one morning with her face aglow with delight. She felt her heart "enlarged," and her "mouth opened" in prayer that morning. As was usual with her at such times, she remembered the lone boy at Crone's Corner, and the lamented wanderer. As she rose from her knees, the thought came to her, as if spoken audibly, "Invite Thomas to your class." Her full heart answered, "I will." It was this which caused her face to glow

and her heart to rejoice. When she told her
mother of this purpose, she mildly suggested
that perhaps Mr. Alden would object. For
a moment Patty's countenance was shaded
with doubt. Then she exclaimed joyfully,
"John Alden's family always agree to any
project which benefits others." * *

There was a very sober joy at Crone's
Corner after the close of the school. Tom's
improved position at the examination, gratified all. Jane and Betsey echoed their
brother's praise as it fell from their parents'
lips. Yet Mr. and Mrs. Crone heard with
a slight feeling of regret Tom's intimations
that he wanted to continue his studies. What
did he want to be studying so much for?
Their life-long narrow views of learning did
not at once give way when their hearts came
into an improved condition. But they were
in a good frame to be instructed. They
now thought that nearly a whole winter's
opportunity to study, in a school so much

better than ever they had, had placed their son on nearly the top of the Hill of Knowledge. And then, how was the farm work to be done by a boy whose head was being crammed with new ideas? He would be spoiled by being above his business. It would be, they argued, a sheer waste of time. Yet, we are pleased to say, Mrs. Crone did not *storm* against it as she once would have done. She only gave it a quiet but decided "cold shoulder."

This greatly burdened Tom. He went about the work of preparing for the spring plowing and planting, with a resolute determination to do his duty to his parents. His studies were pursued in little fractions of time, and slyly, as if he was doing wrong. No boy ever learns much with cowed and burdened spirits, and so he was fast losing his interest in seeking further improvement, and thus in danger of receding from the advanced ground he had taken. Heretofore his parents had done wickedly from reckless passion. Now they simply erred from ignorance, but yet the error was likely to be very serious in its influence upon their boy. His interest in his books when once lost, would leave him exposed to adopt his old, bad habits of employing his little leisure time.

Just at this point in his experience, the arrangement at Alden Farm for its boys, was reported to them. It came through their neighbor, an "Old Maid gossiper," Miss Corner. "Did you ever," said Miss Corner, "see anything beat it! John Alden is sartinly crazy. Deacon Prime thinks as how he is, and the deacon is *never* mistaken."

"What has he been doing now?" inquired Mrs. Crone, with none of her former enthusiasm in such talk. Miss Corner had felt she was losing her influence with the Crones, and she had come, hoping to revive it with her present bit of gossip.

"Why, sartin as you're alive, he's a-going to send his two lazy boys to school all summer! And that isn't the whole on't neither! He's a-going to send 'em to Patty Vose! There now!"

Miss Corner waited for Jerusha Crone's acceptance of her statements, and hearty agreement with her denunciation. But Mrs. Crone simply remarked that maybe there was some mistake, and added, "John Alden's folks are amazing lucky — somehow they do hit on the right way."

Miss Corner was disgusted. She left the house immediately, muttering to herself, "Jerusha has grown so crusty like, since Zeke run away, that I'll never tell her anything again!"

When Mr. and Mrs. Crone learned the facts about the plan for the boys at Alden Farm, it caused them much talk when alone at their fireside. John Alden, they agreed, was very wise. If he was going to encourage the boys to study, most likely that was best. Besides, they learned that his plan was to have them work some every day. "Perhaps," suggested Mr. Crone, "he thinks he will get about as much work out of them as if they wan't encouraged to get learning."

"Yes," said Mrs. Crone, warmly, "when boys *want to study*, it stands to reason that they will be kinder moping, if they don't have a chance."

Silence followed this remark, and both were plainly wandering away to Tom, with painful associations with Zeke.

Tom soon saw the altered bearing of his parents towards his books. He became less shy when he had a book in hand. Gradually he found the way opening for more time for his studies, plainly by his parents' arrangement. His place at the stand was reserved for him, or a candle and table placed apart for his use. The children were hushed, if they were unnecessarily noisy.

No words were spoken, but actions and the spirit which breathes in them are often "winged words."

It was just in this state of things that Patty's invitation to Tom, through his parents, came. The Spirit who had prompted her while in prayer for his guidance, to tender the work of love, had prepared them to receive it.

CHAPTER XIV.

STUDYING BY RULE.

PRISCILLA CODLIN, whose father, it must never be forgotten, was captain of the militia company of the town, had been condescendingly entertaining the question whether she should honor Patty by becoming one of her scholars. She had learned that John Alden's plans were popular in the end; she would therefore be thought to be a partaker of his wisdom. She would, she thought, take private lessons in Latin and Greek, having long since finished her education in the more common studies. But when Priscilla heard that Tom Crone was to be among her pupils, she was amazed. "I *am* astonished!" she exclaimed, throwing up both hands, and turning up her one little pug nose — she would have turned both up if she had owned two — "I am *amazed!*" she added, putting her foot down with emphasis, "at Mr. Alden's want of refinement! Why! did you ever! his children going to a private school with Tom Crone! Well, *I* shall not go, that's settled!"

So it has gone into history — that is the history of the transaction we are writing, — that Miss Priscilla Codlin, daughter of Captain Ichabod Codlin, did not become a pupil of our friend Patty, and for the reason above stated.

The arrangement first made with Patty by Mr. Alden was this: The boys were to spend from ten to twelve A. M., with her, Tuesday and Friday forenoon. They were then to recite such lessons as had been given them, and receive her explanations. He thought this would do to start with. Besides, the spring work was especially pressing, and he desired too, to see, as he expressed it, how hard work and hard study would go together.

At the first meeting of the three boys with their new teacher, the time was spent in a pleasant talk. Miles showed a little impatience at first, under the talk. Why don't she give us our lessons, and explain them, if she's going to, was an expression with which he would have vented his vexation if he had been away from his teacher. But he soon dismissed all uneasiness. Patty was teaching them how to study, and she drew them so gently into her own systematic way that they hardly knew how they came by the resolution to adopt her method. Miles sat down in a corner of the kitchen by himself that evening, and became deeply absorbed in puzzling over something which very much interested him.

"You mean to get your lessons on the sly," said Carver, good naturedly. "Don't get up an ambition to beat Tom and me so soon. Give us a decent chance."

Miles took no notice of this bantering. After another half hour's puzzling, he handed Carver a little slip of paper. It was a plan for the disposal of each of the twenty-four hours. The hour of retiring was to be nine o'clock. That generally had been the hour. They were to rise at four, and study one hour—until five, when the cattle were to be fed, and other work at the barn done, which would take the time until six, the breakfast hour. Then followed the family devotions. Miles put down an hour for breakfast and family prayer. From seven to twelve was set down for work on the farm, as their father might direct; dinner at twelve, and then study until five, when the time to seven was to be absorbed by chores, supper, family prayer, affording two evening hours for study.

Carver laughed heartily at this programme,

but after a few moments he whispered seriously to Miles, "Brother, you didn't put down any time for reading the Bible and secret prayer. You know Patty had Luther's motto in Latin written and hung up over her study table. She told us it meant, 'To pray well is to study well.'"

Miles blushed at the reproof, took his paper and corrected it, by putting in, as Patty had suggested, reading the Bible and prayer on rising, and before retiring, and always prayer before commencing to study.

"There," said Miles, handing the paper back to his brother, and speaking rather lightly, "will that do? It's too pious though, and I shan't live up to it. I'll scratch out the prayer before studying. As to the other, you know, Carve, we always say our prayers when we get up and when we go to bed."

"How about reading the Bible?" suggested Carver.

"Well, don't father read at the family prayers twice a day?" replied Miles, a little petulantly. "Won't that do?"

"I suppose so," said Carver, feeling that he had said more than became him on a matter in reference to which his practice had been no better than his brother's. But Patty's few words on the subject of private prayer and reading the Scriptures in connection with study, given with modesty and great tenderness, had deeply impressed the older brother. He yielded to his brother's thoughtless remark on not being too pious about the matter, while he secretly resolved that he would give more attention to it.

A few days' experiment taught Miles that he could not calculate quite so closely. One morning little Jeremiah was quite sick, and the breakfast hour was delayed, and for the same reason the dinner was not eaten until one o'clock. Another morning was put into disorder by the boys themselves. They slept soundly until their father called them at five o'clock.

"A plague take it!" said Miles, when he saw the lateness of the hour. "It's no use to be systematic. It only bothers a fellow to try."

Carver laughed, and took the matter very coolly. "We'll soon make it up," he remarked, as he dressed very deliberately.

"No, we shan't," persisted Miles. "We may chase this hour all day, and not catch it."

Some special calls would occasionally compel their father to break over his own arrangement of allowing the boys the afternoon. Nor was the evening always at their disposal. Their place of study was one corner of the great kitchen, which, thanks to the stove, always aglow, was as comfortable as any part of the room. But callers sometimes spent an hour or more, talking so loud and incessantly, that their heads became confused.

So at the end of a few days, Miles took his programme and wrote on the bottom in large letters, "Studying by rule is all a humbug! (signed) Miles Alden." He pushed the paper along to Carver the next morning just as they were sitting down to their books at half-past four.

Carver took it, and wrote beneath Miles' signature, in a bolder hand, "Studying without rule is a greater humbug. (Signed) Carver Alden."

Miles acknowledged himself hit, but he did not exactly see the point. But nothing more was said. Both were soon so deeply absorbed in their lessons, that they had to be reminded by their mother that, "Certain creatures in the barn wonder if the rules of Alden Farm are not being broken to their annoyance." The boys needed only this hint. They scampered off to the barn almost too promptly to catch the last word, "annoyance." But Miles did hear it, and exclaimed, as they entered the barn, half playfully and half in earnest, "I guess 'rules' annoy somebody besides cattle and horses."

"No rules would be worse," insisted Carver.

* * * * *

Hope Cottage was a little nearer Crone's Corner than it was to Alden Farm. Tom was promptly in his place on recitation days. His lessons were not so perfectly learned as were those of his schoolmates. Yet his teacher greeted him with words of encouragement only. The Alden boys had towards him all of the cordial good will which they had cultivated during the winter. To an old friend who bantered Miles on having a *Crone* for a school fellow, he showed something like resentment. "Tom's company is as good as yours any day!" was the tart reply. It alienated for many months old friends, and Miles regretted it, and finally restored good feeling, by a manly apology.

To a more proving taunt, Carver had a better answer. "If Tom is better than we are," he replied, with that independence which belonged to the Aldens, "we shall be lifted up a piece by his influence. If he is below us, we shall lift him up, and that will be still pleasanter."

"There's no getting round John Alden's boys," said the teaser, and walked away. But candor requires us to say that Carver quoted the substance of this remark from Patty, though the application of it to Tom was his own.

Tom's lessons, we stated, were not quite as perfectly learned as were those of the other boys. He had copied Miles' rules for systemizing study time. But things were much less orderly at the Corner than at the Farm. Although his parents had consented to give him the same time for his books which was granted to his two friends, it was subject to almost constant interruption.

He became much disturbed — sometimes he was vexed and discouraged. He did not write down in large letters, "Studying by rule is a humbug," but he often exclaimed, "It's no use." Besides, Tom was constantly oppressed by a sense of his loneliness. "If Zeke was only here," he would involuntarily say to himself, and when he saw Carver and Miles coming bounding along together towards Hope Cottage on recitation day, he wiped the unbidden tear from his pensive face.

The parents of Tom encouraged their boy just as much as they knew how. To them it was an effort of parental sacrifice and duty, in an unpractised direction. They earnestly desired the "good luck" of Alden Farm in their children, and they were now, according to their small ability, willing to pay the price it demanded. They were "ceasing to do evil, and learning to do well," and God was daily increasing both their strength and pleasure in the good way.

In the meantime the blunders of Tom's parents, which nearly upset all the good there was in him, were offset by Patty's steady hand, and her keen perception both of Tom's wants and their proper supply.

Miles, one day, in his good-natured, bluff way, pushed his programme for study, with its emphatic additions over his and Carver's names, under the eye of Patty. She read it all, and then looked at the boys with one of her meaning smiles.

"There's something coming about that programme," whispered Miles to Carver, laying down his book, and looking Patty attentively in the face.

"I have had large experience on this subject for one no older than I am," said Patty. "And," she added, with a merry twinkle of her eye, which always made the boys merry too, "I believe with Miles, that studying by rule is a humbug—"

Miles fairly jumped from his seat, clapping his hands with delight, to think that his teacher had indorsed his emphatic note. Carver and Tom laughed, of course, for Patty's merry face said they might, but they were a little puzzled to understand what Patty could mean, since she had prompted some such programme by her remarks on being "very regular" in all that was undertaken, "saving every moment of time possible." When the laugh was subsided, Patty continued, more seriously, by saying, "and I believe with Carver, that no rules for study are a greater humbug!"

It was Carver's turn now to laugh outright, which he did, with a knowing glance at Miles.

"A plan of study," continued the teacher, "is a humbug, especially for boys situated as you are, which has not a large margin for necessary interruptions. Very persistent boys who make them, fret when they fail to be able to keep them. It plagues them dreadfully."

"It annoys them as it does the cows to have a late breakfast," whispered Miles.

"They are not willing," continued the teacher, "that their parents should call them away from their books, however great the necessity for doing so. They feel like being disobedient, or what is about the same thing, they want to stop, and say, 'I don't want to. I shouldn't think you would make me. I shall *never* get my lesson.' Or they get discouraged, and say, 'It's no use!'"

"That's me," said Tom to himself.

"I would rather have you adopt this rule," added Patty, her face becoming at once more serious and animated in its expression, "establish a habit of improving *every* moment in some useful way. When duty or necessity does not call another way, give it to study. A will in study which settles us into a pleasant, easy habit of sitting down to a book when duty does not call us in another way, makes itself a rule. And what is of priceless value, makes it pleasant for us *not* to study, if duty forbids it."

The boys had settled into the most sober attention before Patty had closed these remarks. Tom's countenance lost its shade of sadness. Miles gazed at his teacher with a look which said, 'I understand you — I see it now!' and Carver folded his arms and assumed a thoughtful attitude. Patty dropped her voice and added at the close of her remarks, pointing to Luther's motto hung upon the wall, "Remember always, my young friends, that 'To have prayed well is to have studied well.'"

The boys scampered home, frisky as young colts, and light of heart as the uncaged spring birds. The Aldens, "just for the fun of it," they said, accompanied Thomas to the gateway leading to his home. Then with exclamations, shouted out with a hearty good will, "Good bye, Tom!" "Success to you!" "Be on hand next Friday!" they turned their faces and run home.

Mrs. Croné came to the doorway just in time to see the cordial good will at parting, and to hear the farewell shouts. Tom bounded up the path with a "How d'ye do, mother?" and a "What can I do for you first?"

The whole scene impressed itself so upon the mother's now tender feelings, as contrasted with the too frequent manner of the meeting of boys and mother in the past, that she buried her face in her checked apron and burst into tears. Tom, thinking he had in some way wounded his mother's feelings, approached her timidly with words of apology. She at once dropped her apron, and threw her arms about his neck and kissed him, weeping the while like a child. This turn of affairs at once enabled Tom to understand the spirit of the occasion. It was a new inspiration of effort in the right way. It thrilled his heart, and, added to Patty's winning ways, made him strong to endure, and willing to act, in the pathway of duty.

CHAPTER XV.

MOSE POND.

THE spring was fading off into summer. The ground, mellowed by the plough, harrow and hoe, had received its seed. The birds were less engaged in song, and more with their nests, around which they hovered, looking with pride and tender care at their contents. The Alden boys had, by permission, devoted their field working hours, for a few weeks, to the little farm at Hope Cottage. Patty often came out with her great sun-bonnet, beneath which her little form seemed hid away, and out from under which her bright eyes shone like sunbeams in pearly dew drops. Miles insisted that their teacher, on such occasions, "was real bewitching." "I tell you what it is, Carver," he would say, "Patty *is* handsome — she's the prettiest girl in this town."

"She is the smartest and best," was Carver's sober reply.

The little cultivated patches about the Cottage were beginning to show plainly the springing seed which had been planted. The trees of the orchard had been nicely rid of caterpillars, which were Patty's detestation. Her often expressed faith that God had made nothing in vain, was severely tried when she saw a huge nest of these little creatures, from which slimy tracks might be traced over every tender limb and twig. Her part had been to point them out when the new race were yet in the egg, and Miles had made quick and thorough work with them, by crushing them in his gloved hand.

Patty herself had made and planted the flower beds, some of which were full of beauty and sweet perfume.

Besides what they had done at the Cottage farm, the Alden boys had been worth at home, as their father said, in his spirited way, "A dozen mopes, who were dragging about the farm because they were compelled to work." They had made pleasure of their duty. The neighbors were very critical in their examination of the Alden Farm, this spring, to see how its owner's experiment was working. But the croakers found no capital for their grumbling. Everything was in order, as usual. His fields were among the most thrifty looking. His orchards were well trimmed, and cleaned of their enemies. No barns were in tidier order. No stock looked better satisfied, or spoke better words for their owner.

William Treat, whose life, long one of drifting down the Broad Way, but had been one, since the husking, which looked heavenward, declared, in his enthusiasm for his good friend Alden, that his fowls cackled and crowed more joyously than any others. Treat's old companion in sin, Mose Pond,— still about always drunk with "moderate drinking," came and leaned upon the fence of John Alden's corn-field. He knew how it had always looked, but he had hoped to find the fences down, and the weeds towering above the corn. "Lucky fellow, is this John Alden!" muttered Mose. "I be blamed if his corn wouldn't grow and the weeds die, if he, and his stuck-up boys didn't do nothing. It always was his luck. *My* corn won't grow. It never would, and all John Alden's weeds are just mean enough to move off his premises and stick themselves down on my planting. I be blamed if they don't! And this here fence of John's — why a thousand tornadoes couldn't start a strip of it" — and Moses clinched the innocent fence, and, bracing his feet, jerked and twisted this way and that, with drunken fury, to prove that *he* could do what a tornado could not. Suddenly the fence gave way. Down Mose rolled full eight feet, until he reached the bottom of the banking. "It wouldn't a sarved John Alden so, nor none of his stuck-up, go to school boys!" said Mose, picking himself up, and brushing the dust from his eyes, and spitting the dirt from his mouth. "You mean thing, you," added Mose, giving the board a kick, "go tell yer owner to nail yer tighter next time, so yer can stand a fellow's heft."

There was so little comfort to the drunken idler in looking at John Alden's fields, that he staggered down, the next day, to Crone's Corner. He had heard that his boy too had got "high notions." He knew too that one boy "was not." He felt certain of comfort here in seeing neglected fields, fallen fences, and a desponding farmer. He had not quite reached the Corner before his legs gave out. He said, "They'd been weak like for some time, and he had taken his "mod-crate" glass that very morning to strengthen them. It was strange, he thought, they did not hold out. He laid it, however, to the *smallness* of the glass. As he sat, or, rather lay, under the fence, a boon companion came along, who was also afflicted with leg weakness.

"It's no use," said his companion, "to go down to see Zeke. I've been."

"Temperance folks well nigh ruined him, hey?" said Mose.

"No, he and Jerusha's real stuck up."

"They've run young Zeke off, though," said Mose; "I ollers shall believe John Alden's folks run him off. They's got 'tother boy off too under Patty Vose's sun-bonnet! Old Zeke's farm looks like crazy, hey?"

"Never looked half so well! Blamed if it did! All the temperance folks got luck this year! Old Zeke has jined 'em. He wouldn't wet a fellow's whistle if it was to save him."

Mose turned his unsteady steps homeward. It was his last visit, or attempted visit to the fields of his neighbors. He fell at his own gate-way as he had often done before. His wife and children ran from him instead of towards him, when he fell. But his groans soon brought them to his relief. They lifted him up, and the blood flowed freely down his face. He had struck his temple against a sharp stone. Moses Pond's "moderate" drinking had given him so many falls and cuts which had caused his bad blood to flow, that very little was thought of this affair by his family. But no sooner had they stopped the flow of blood, than a wild start or frantic gesture started it again. Dr. Burt was finally sent for. The flow of blood was prevented, but the patient became uncontrollably delirious. His ravings were frightful to his family, beyond any former experience. "See! see!" he exclaimed, staring at a fancied object in the corner of the room.

"Take them away! take them away, won't you! Don't anybody care! They'll claw me to death! Take them off, I say!" he screamed with great violence.

Utterly exhausted at last, Mose fell into a quiet sleep. When he awoke he stared about, as if to assure himself that he was with his family. "It's you, Eunice, is it?" he said, addressing his wife.

"Yes, dear, it is your own wife."

"Come here, Becky," he said to his oldest child, a girl about ten years old. Rebecca approached timidly, as if in doubt whether her father was drunk or sober. He stretched out his feeble hand and drew her to his face and kissed her. The child looked confused. She had been often struck and kicked, and but seldom kissed. He called Jennie, the only other child, a sickly girl of four years. He stroked her flaxen hair tenderly, kissed her and wept freely. Then looking up into his wife's face, he said, in sobbing accents, "My dear, can you ever forgive me?"

No such tender words had she heard from him since he had become a noisy advocate of "moderate drinking." She knelt by his bed-side and wet her penitent husband's face with her tears.

"Eunice, I must die, but tell me, can you forgive me?"

"Yes, dear husband, I do, but you must not die. You must live to comfort us."

"I must die, Eunice," he said, more feebly.

"Shall I send for your good friend, Deacon Prime?" inquired his wife. The dying man shook his head, and whispered, "Curtis — John "—

"The minister?"

"Y-e-s, and J-o-h-n."

"John Alden?" said his wife.

He nodded assent, and sunk back upon his pillow, scarcely giving signs of life.

The minister and John Alden were soon

present, and both pray'ed fervently and tenderly for God's mercy to be granted, through Jesus Christ, "even as to the thief upon the cross." Moses opened his eyes and looked with apparent consciousness upon Mr. Alden, as if his last thoughts were of the great truths of religion which he had so often urged in vain upon his attention, and then closed them in death.

* * * * *

Moses Pond was buried quietly, as was fitting he should be, from his own home, now full of mourning, but not more desolate than his life had made it. The next Sabbath a solemn and large audience listened to the words of the faithful pastor. He closed his sermon with tender entreaty to all, especially to the young, to give their hearts to God — to turn from every evil way, especially that of the intoxicating cup. "I warn you," added the preacher, with a fervor that melted the congregation, "against the *first glass!* The time has fully come!" he exclaimed, with a tone of authority, "to declare that total abstinence is the only temperance."

There was a commotion in the parish the following week. Dr. Burt demanded a parish meeting to consider the pastor's heresy of faith on the temperance question. He went about arguing warmly that *he* had not been the cause of Mose Pond's dreadful death, though nobody accused him. "Mose," he declared everywhere, "would take too much in spite of all my faithful and kind warnings. I *knew* he took too much and told him so. Am *I* to blame because he died a drunkard?"

John Alden now roused himself, like a lion whose lair is invaded by the hunters. He held temperance meetings in every neighborhood in town, the people flocking to hear him, and signing the pledge.

Patty said she never wanted so much to

be a minister. But she thanked God that her minister was on the right track. She at once set herself at work to do what she could in her own way. She had three at least trusty servants at her command. She reckoned them a host. She gave her three scholars a prompting to get up a boys' temperance society.

"What can we do?" inquired Tom, timidly.

"You can do a great deal!" said Patty, with spirit. Then suddenly checking her earnestness, she added, in a lower, gentle tone, "I mean if you seek divine help. How I wish my boys knew *how* to pray aright."

Patty wrote for the boys a pledge, and gave each a copy. They agreed to see, before many weeks, every boy in town. They divided off the town into districts, and each took an assigned territory. As the boys were going out, after having received their pledges, Miles lingered for a moment behind. There was a half serious, half comical expression about his face, not uncommon with him.

"Well, Miles," said Patty, approaching him in her gentle, loving way, "what do you wish to say?"

"Can't you, teacher, do the praying about this business, while we do the work?" whispered Miles. "I don't think we boys can any how."

Having freed his mind, Miles did not wait for an answer. He soon overtook Carver and Tom, and the three talked over their plans about the new enterprise. They thought they knew the name and residence of every boy in town. So they agreed to write them down that evening. The Aldens generously offered to take a part of those assigned to Tom, for they saw he was quite timid about the business.

Tom told his mother at once, what Patty had proposed for her scholars to do.

She received the statement quite coldly at

first. Her son's courage, never great, went down to utter cowardice. "I can't," struggled for utterance. In the mother's mind there was a conflict. Old, narrow views were warring with new and better ones. Her husband felt in the same manner, though he waited for his wife to declare her feeling. The fireside talk, just before retiring, brought the matter to a decision.

"I should think," said Mrs. Crone, "that Tom had enough to do already."

"I should think so," replied her husband. There was a moment's silence.

"It would do Tom good, I suppose," remarked Mrs. Crone, dreamily.

"It certainly would," said Mr. Crone.

Another pause, and Mrs. Crone remarked, "The Alden boys will do it all if he don't. They'll have all the boys with them too, I'll warrant. Aldens can always make folks go with them, and I wonder why *our* boy can't do something as well as they!"

"I should think he might," said Ezekiel Crone, decisively.

The parents having reached a satisfactory conclusion on the matter, the mother reported to Tom accordingly. Tom's courage went up again. He had just that timid nature which needed sympathy, and wanted courage breathed into him from a stronger nature. Then he could work well in a good cause — work persistently, and reap for himself and others a harvest. He and Miles were, as Patty said, good complements for each other. Miles liked sympathy, but neither sought it nor depended upon it. A little opposition was a spur to his resolution. He had strong convictions, and a will strong enough to act up to them.

Tom put unusual energy into his part of the farm work, and every time he went out with his paper for "signers," he came back with greater self-respect and moral power. If at any time his heart was growing faint under an unexpected rebuff, when he "compared notes" with Miles, he was strong again. One day as he was arguing for total abstinence and the pledge, a special friend and disciple of Doctor Burt broke in upon his talk. His name was Green. He was about ten years older than Tom.

"Look here, now, you young meddler," said Green, breaking in upon Tom's conversation, "you talk like a ninny. What do you know about the matter any way? Do you know more than all the doctors? Dr. Burt has studied at college. He's got larnin'. He says a little liquor's good for a man, and an't all our fathers used it — the ministers, and all good folks! Now, it isn't likely they'd a used it if it was such an awful bad thing. You're trying to get away the rights of the boys by that are pledge."

Tom modestly suggested that every drunkard began by taking a little; that when people began to drink it was not easy to take only a little, nor to leave off when they found it hurt them. He cited Mose Pond's case, as an illustration of the evils of moderate drinking.

Tom had good arguments, and Green a loud voice and a bad temper. When Tom named Pond, Green exclaimed, shaking his fist in Tom's face, "Tom Crone, you're a fool! All the Crones are fools, and always was!" To these insults Green added a violent push, saying, as Tom went reeling against the fence, "What do you think yourself to be? Sich as you trying to tell folks when they ought to drink!"

Tom pursued his mission work no further that day. It was his first experience in a violent return of evil for his good. He had not learned to rejoice at it, nor to feel that it was for Christ's sake. He did not recover from the disheartening blow until he had received the sympathy of his mother and of the Aldens. When Miles heard Tom's story concerning his contact with Green, Miles shrugged his shoulders, saying, "Mean to hunt up Green next time I go out, wouldn't you, Carver?"

"Don't know as I should," replied Carver. "You will cast your pearls before swine, maybe."

"Oh, it's not a pearl I am going to throw at him," said Miles, laughing.

"What will you throw at him?"

"Hard arguments."

"And what if he laughs at them?"

"Why, I'll let him laugh."

"But what more than argments will you use with Green?"

"Facts."

"Father says facts are the best kind of arguments," added Carver.

"Yes," replied Miles, with a significant nod of his head, "especially when they hit as hard as mine will hit Green."

The boys separated. There was something

in the defiant spirit of Miles toward Green that made Tom ashamed that he had allowed so worthless a fellow, who so meanly defended a bad cause, to burden him. "I wish I did have more courage when I *know* I'm right," he said to himself, as he walked thoughtfully home.

Miles found no difficulty in meeting Green. He found him where he was generally to be found, lounging about the grocery store stables. Green's triumph over Tom was so easy in his own estimation, that he counted on an equally easy task in sending home abashed any temperance boy. He was becoming very insolent, and a great hindrance to the further circulation of the pledge among the young folks. Miles commenced his efforts to get pledges in the presence of this defiant advocate of rum. Green at once strode towards him, and began his denunciation of all teetotalism. He rehearsed the old argument of a little being good for one, and sneered at *boys* pretending to know "more'n the doctors," and being "wiser than all the fathers."

"How much *is* 'a little rum'?" said Miles.

"Why, as much as will do a man good."

"How much will do a man good, hey?"

"Why — yes — as much as makes him feel better. I don't believe, you see, in getting drunk."

"Just so much as Mose Pond always had — only just enough to make him feel better. *He* never had too much, in his own judgment."

"Mose was a fool, and so are you."

Not regarding the personal insult, Miles confronted Green with an unflinching bravery, and demanded, in a clear, strong, unfaltering voice, "Do *you* know what a little is? — do *you* know when you get enough?"

"Yes," was the faltering reply, as Green looked upon Miles' honest, bold face and searching eye, and upon the crowd of boys who had gathered about them, all of whom knew his habits well.

"Yes, *sir*," replied Miles, in a voice so vociferous that he made every boy in the crowd feel the force of his reply—"Yes, *sir*, you knew exactly what was enough when you lay under the wall drunk last Saturday night! You have known just how much is a *little*, for twelve months, and been drunk all of twelve times!"

"You're a mean temperance meddler!" exclaimed Green, in a passion, drawing back and raising his arm defiantly.

Miles stood on the defensive, without flinching.

"A fight! a fight!" shouted the boys. "Give 'em fair play." Green was much the older, but Miles' well developed muscles, large and strong limbs, showed that he had at least, a tolerable chance, if the dispute came to blows, and it was evident it would if Green struck the first blow. In fact, he rather desired to humble the advocate of rum by a sound whipping. It was plain he had left the praying to Patty, and had assumed a little more of the acting than was becoming in a moral reform.

"Better not strike an Alden," said a voice in the crowd. "Miles will lay you out stiffer than a poker."

Green thought discretion the better part of valor, and beat a hasty retreat, amidst the jeers of the crowd. His influence with the boys was gone.

CHAPTER XVI.

A NEW LIFE.

GREAT success crowned the efforts of Patty's scholars, so that she was more than ever esteemed by their parents. Mr. Alden called what had been done among the young, "Patty's work," for she devised the plan of operation, and directed and sustained by her wisdom and courage, the efforts. It became the "town's talk." The sober, thoughtful people, for the most part rejoiced. The Dr. Burt party, aided by the liquor sellers and all the drunkards, talked loud, and with *awful* solemnity. "What are we coming to?" said the grocery store loafers. "Women and the boys are a-going to take away our rights."

The movement among the children had

nowhere done more good than at the Corner. Mr. and Mrs. Crone were greatly benefited by Tom's connection with it. It had enlarged their range of thought with regard to their boy. They had valued their children by the measure of their usefulness in the work of their hands. Having never felt to any great extent responsibility for the moral good of others, they never thought of such a line of service for their children. Tom's labors had greatly benefited them in this respect. They were conscious of a higher and broader estimate of character. The Spirit whispered through this incident, "Go work in my vineyard!"

As to Tom, it was a marked era in his life — the most important he had ever seen. He labored on the farm with more heart, for he had greater self-respect. He felt that he was already somebody. He studied easier and with more pleasure, for he had a nobler aim.

* * * * *

The summer was now ended. The farmers were in the midst of their harvest work. The pupils of Patty recited good lessons, up to the commencement of the harvesting, except during a vacation in the warm weeks of dogdays. They now gave their whole time to the farms. They were happy in the thought that no summer had been so full of pleasure and improvement. They were in danger indeed of being too full of self-confidence. Miles especially, put on some "airs." His triumph over Green obtained him many compliments. While his conduct towards Tom was full of his characteristic kindness, his bearing was becoming that of a superior. Carver was less vain but more proud. He did not talk as freely of himself as his brother did, nor attempt to "show off," but he entertained the conviction that Carver Alden of Alden Farm, had few equals and no superiors. He thought with great satisfaction of the future day when he should be in college, and show the wondering students what he could do! The private character of the boys' school encouraged these feelings. They measured themselves by themselves, and were not wise. They needed, for a correction of these errors, the healthful competition of a large school, gathered from a wide range of country, some of whose scholars might take the vanity and pride out of them.

The harvesting at Alden's and at the Corner was never more abundant for the labor bestowed; and it is certain that "harvest home," was never sung more joyfully. Only one cloud — that, a dark, heavy one — hung over the now truly Christian home of Ezekiel Crone.

The feelings of Mr. Alden, over whose family joy no cloud hung, are well expressed in the following incident. The product of his fields had all been gathered into his barns and granaries. Thanksgiving day, with its fullness of occasion to praise the God of harvest, had passed. He had given of his abundance with a liberal hand to the poor. Still, the yearning of the hearts of the parental heads of the Alden family was to do more for the Master.

It was when they were just in this state of feeling that their pastor, Mr. Curtis, and his wife, favored them with an evening's visit. Two topics of conversation were of absorbing interest, until an unusually late hour. One was joyous, and the other sad. "The signs of the outpourings of God's spirit," said Mr. Curtis, "were never so encouraging. The bow of promise is in the parting clouds. The temperance reform has cleared the moral atmosphere by removing in a great degree, an old, scandalous stumbling-block."

"I believe you are right," replied Mr. Alden, with animation. "The young people were never more seriously disposed. Their attention to the words preached was never better!" He closed this strain of remark by saying, solemnly, "Oh, that God would add to His great mercies to my family this one: the conversion of my children!"

It was arranged between the pastor and his faithful member, to secure an agreement on the part of all the earnest, spiritual members, to meet on Thursday afternoon of each week, in the great kitchen of the parsonage, to pray for this one thing, — the gift of larger measures of the Spirit. Patience and Mrs. Curtis entered warmly into the proposal. They began immediately to stir up the sisters in the good work.

The sad topic of conversation was the sickness of Deacon Prime, of which Mr. Alden had not heard. He had been repelled from the society and fellowship of this aged office bearer. No "misunderstanding" had ever occurred, more than that which came naturally out of great difference both of views on many religious topics, and of Christian experience.

The deacon's godliness had been one of undoubted sincerity, but it was very sour. The law with him was more than the gospel; he had taken it not as "a schoolmaster to bring him to Christ," but as the bearer of a scourge with which to chastise the "old man" into the image and nature of the "new man." But Mr. Alden resolved to go at once and tender his Christian condolence to his brother. But when calling upon the devout and Christlike Deacon Turner, he thought best to delay his visit. The pastor and the younger deacon had been more than once, and found their aged brother in a state of great conflict of mind. A change, they thought, was coming over him. It would be best to wait.

We will visit Deacon Prime's sick room, and he shall speak for himself. The deacon's sickness assumed, from the first, a serious character. He was impressed that his departure was near. He began to listen to the reading of the Bible with a deeper interest. He had read it morning and evening for many years, but now its utterances seemed clothed with fresh authority.

"I have been a great sinner," said the deacon, sighing deeply. His family turned to the precious promises, especially those which fell from Christ's own lips. His burdened heart saw *only* the fact that he was a sinner. There was no comfort in the view, but increasing distress. Good Deacon Turner came in, and pressed upon his attention, and held before his mind the atoning blood. He urged as the sole ground of the sinner's acceptance, "Repentance towards God, and faith towards our Lord Jesus Christ,"—a doctrine the despairing deacon had always held and pressed upon others. "To him that *believeth*," said Deacon Turner fervently, "Christ is precious." A night of spiritual darkness followed. In the morning the deacon was bolstered up, and the Word of God was placed before him. He began with Christ's discourse to his disciples, at the institution of the Supper. He was struck with the tenderness of the address, "Let not your heart be troubled, neither let it be afraid. Ye believe in God, believe also in me." He read these words over again. He took off his glasses, wiped them, re-adjusted them, and read them again. They seemed so new he could hardly persuade himself that they were the same words which he had often read from his youth. The Holy Spirit wonderfully illuminated them; and by his aid his heart took hold of the Redeemer who spoke them for every sin-stained but broken and contrite heart. He was no longer troubled. He had always believed in God, whom he saw as "angry with the sinner every day;" he now believed "also" in him "by whose stripes we are healed." His countenance was lighted with holy joy, as he lay breathing a low, tender, fervent utterance of praise. His family felt the change, and greatly rejoiced. His brother in office stood at the bedside with thankfulness and wonder. His pastor saw in the change another evidence of a coming gracious visitation.

"Now," said Deacon Prime, "send for Brother Alden." As he approached his bed, he threw his arms about his neck, and wept freely. "I have been all wrong, Brother Alden. We have held to the same God and the same Saviour, but we have had a different experience. I have wronged you by my words and spirit. I will not *ask* your forgiveness; I read it already in your face. I know by your long cherished, loving spirit that I have it. Oh, that I could live to tell all of the precious love of the Saviour to me."

The deacon ceased, folded his hands across his breast, and fell asleep in Christ. A heavenly smile, which he had never worn in life, settled upon his face in death.

A fresh inspiration was given to the faith

of the praying band, which met at the parsonage on Thursday afternoon. The prayers at 'many family altars were quickened; less formality and more of the spirit of supplication prevailed generally in the parish of Mr. Curtis. "Our children! May they be gathered into Christ's fold!" was the devout exclamation of many parents. While others, sincerely distrusting all professed conversions among young people, turned coldly towards efforts in this direction. The earnest pastor was not one of these; his prayers were never more fervent than when his only child, Jane, was remembered before God.

John and Patience Alden had long ago discussed, in their earnest, thoughtful, independent and prayerful manner, the question of early conversions. It was when their first born was yet a child, that the following talk about this matter occurred.

"Patience," said John, who had just returned from Carver's sleeping-room, where he had tucked him up snugly in his little trundle bed, "Patience, at what age may we rightly expect the conversion of our boy?"

"Just as soon as he may be held responsible for what he does," replied Patience, decidedly.

"It's a great thing to be a Christian," suggested John.

"Certainly," said Patience.

"Conversion is a great work, and children may easily be deceived in such great matters," further suggested Mr. Alden, who was evidently at his well practiced device, of bringing up objections to call out the thoughts of his wife.

"Now, John," said Patience, with an earnestness which startled her husband, "I believe that a child, at his first responsible moments, will more easily and more clearly see Christ as a Saviour, and believe on Him unto salvation, more readily, if properly instructed, than at any later time!"

"Why, Patience!" exclaimed her husband, really surprised at this bold assertion.

"Don't the Spirit strive more earnestly for the child than for the older person who has grieved Him often?" said Patience, with increasing warmth.

"Does He?" inquired Mr. Alden.

"Does a father," said Patience, "ask the acceptance by a child of a favor, more freely after it has been often refused?"

"But we have been taught not to encourage children to expect renewing grace," replied Mr. Alden, hesitatingly.

"But Christ has said, 'Suffer little children to come unto me,'" answered Patience, in a sad tone. She was thinking of her own little faith in a truth she had so earnestly advocated.

Her husband, having obtained what he sought, his wife's clear statements, added to her arguments others in the same direction, and shortly after, at the family altar, thanked

God for the promise that for the little children even, was the kingdom of heaven.

Years had passed since this incident, but now, when the desire for their children's conversion was burdening them, they were greatly humbled that their prayers, labors and faith had been so little in accordance with their expressed belief. The family altar at Alden Farm never breathed more fervent prayers than were now ascending from it. The place of secret prayer witnessed confessions, penitential tears and believing supplications.

"Carve," said the unsuspecting Miles, "how good to us everybody seems!"

"What!" said Carver, looking up from his book.

"How kind everybody is!" repeated Miles. "How father does pray, too!"

"Hasn't he always prayed," said Carver, affecting an indifference to the subject he did not feel. Both boys commenced studying again. They were alone in their parents' sleeping-room, where a fire was occasionally made for them when callers were expected in the kitchen. But their minds were not absorbed in their books as usual. Soon Miles commenced again on the subject which was burdening his heart, but of which he had not courage to speak directly. "How *very* kind Patty is!" he said, as if talking to himself.

"Why, hasn't she always been kind?" said Carver.

"I mean, how *loving* she is," answered Miles.

Carver smiled, and said, "Well, I think she has always been loving."

Miles blushed, but said, resolutely, "I think, Carver, that father and mother, and our teacher want us to be Christians, right off! I see it in their faces all the time. They pray too, that we may, I know they do. Yesterday at the recitation, while you were looking out a word in the Latin Dictionary, Patty rested her elbow on the table and put her face in her hand. She was praying for you, I know she was, for she looked at you so tenderly when you began to translate, and I saw her wipe a tear from one corner of her eye! But I wonder she never talks to us about being Christians. I wish she would say something about Jesus."

Carver made no bluff reply to this. He said nothing, but his brother saw that he was affected, and he followed up his advantage, in the frank expression of a full soul. "Carver," he said, with a choked utterance, "I mean to *try* to give my heart to God."

Both boys bowed their heads upon their study table in silence. Carver had really felt the drawings of God's Spirit longer and more deeply than his brother. But his will was less yielding, and his proud heart warred against the Love which was drawing him to the narrow path of peace and safety. The contention in the heart of Miles was sharper and sooner ended. He wept freely, and finally retired to his own room to weep and pray alone.

While Jesus was thus meeting with Patty's students, and preparing their hearts for the message from Him which might be sent, he spake by His Spirit to her that night. In her oft repeated prayer for her pupils, she had prayed for wisdom in winning them to Christ. Suddenly she now cried out, "Jesus, forgive me; that I have not borne to them the message of thy love more faithfully. I will, by thy help, when next I see them."

The recitations were ended on the following Friday, when Patty, with a fluttering heart, said, "My young friends, would you like to tarry a short time, that we may talk about the Saviour? I want you to give Him your hearts."

Thomas Crone looked into the faces of his Alden friends. He was glad to read there a cordial response to the teacher's request. The words which the faithful teacher uttered dropped like seed into good ground. The Great Sower had been there before her, preparing the ground, by the fertilizing warmth of His Spirit, and by the hammer of His Word breaking its stony hardness. At the close of the interview, all kneeled in brokenness of heart, while the teacher asked for a genuine penitence and faith.

Very little studying was done for several days. Carver and Miles told all their feelings, without embarrassment, to their mother. In her simple Christian discipline she had possessed so much of the Christ Spirit, that no barrier was raised between her and their fullest confidence. Even the rougher nature of their father was childlike simplicity here, and both parents and children, as one family in Christ, talked, sang, and prayed together daily. Patience pointed out to them such passages of Scripture as she deemed specially adapted to their case. She warned them of errors which, as she had learned by experience, beset the seeker's path. Under such guidance and prayers, gradually the peace of the believer entered their hearts.

About three weeks after these incidents, both Carver and Miles were again in their parents' chamber, before a blazing fire, about to commence an evening's study. Both, without concert, had stolen away into their own chamber, for a few moments of secret prayer before commencing. As they were seated at their study table, with books opened before them, Carver looked up and said, seriously, "Miles, we know now what Patty meant when she talked to us about Luther's motto, don't we?"

"Yes," said Miles, smiling, "I think I shan't now want to leave the praying before study, to Patty."

Lonely Thomas Crone groped more in the dark, and through a longer path, to find the

Light of Life. His instruction in religious things had been very limited. He had never felt any freedom in talking with his parents about holy things; and even now, when both were very glad to see his seriousness, and evident desire to love the Saviour, they did not know what to say to him. They saw and felt this, and were greatly humbled. "Ezekiel," said Mrs. Crone, as she looked into Tom's beseeching countenance, "Ezekiel, we ought to be teachers in divine things, but we are only babes. God forgive us, and make our boy a Christian, and a better one, too, than we have been."

But Tom found in his teacher and schoolmates, willing helpers, and he too, was soon happy in the peace which passes understanding, and the joy which is full of the Holy Ghost.

CHAPTER XVII.

BURDENED HEARTS.

THE awakening had reached the home of Joel Organ, the father of Fred. As we have stated, they lived on a by-road several miles from town. Mr. Organ's wife, Mary, never possessed of an amiable disposition, had been more than ever ill-tempered since the mysterious disappearance of Zeke Crone. She manifested strange emotions when the continued mourning of his parents for him was mentioned by a caller. She would at once break out into a noisy talk about it. "Why," she exclaimed, "should Jerusha Crone, or her old man, care for Zeke's loss? He *can't* be worse off than he was at home. They drove him out doors, and so who's to blame! They needn't tell *me* that they do care anything about it! I know 'em! For my part, I think they may thank anybody who has given Zeke a shelter."

This heat was exciting attention and causing remarks. Mrs. Organ saw this, and shut herself up in her obscure home more than ever. Fred was removed from school soon after his mean conduct towards Thomas Crone. He had been allowed to go to town but little, and even Mr. Organ's visits were jealously restrained by his wife. Thus shut out from society, they were little likely to be partakers of the religious interest of the town. But the Holy Spirit can not be shut out from the by-ways of sin when he is moved towards them by earnest, believing prayer. We will note how it was.

Patty Vose rejoiced with a cautious, deep interest, in the evidence of a saving change in her pupils. It was not with her as with many Christians when dear friends are converted. Her solicitude did not *cease* with their conversion. She knew that their Christian life was but just begun; that there were conflicts through which they must pass, and work for them to do; that they needed to be built up in the faith of Jesus, and to grow in grace; and that they needed for all this the counsel of experience, and the guidance of older Christians. So they had been her pupils, not only in Greek and Latin, but in the more important things of holy living. "The luck of Alden Farm" was never more apparent than in the religious growth of its boys, so Patty's work in reference to them, was the comparatively easy one of co-operation. But for Thomas Crone her labor was more responsible and difficult. His parents did little for his Christian culture. How could they impart that of which they had obtained so little! They felt their lack keenly. "John Alden's boys will be sure to hold out," said Mrs. Crone.

"Everything he and Patience undertake comes out right. They've been always lucky. Our boy has got to stumble along, I suppose, just as his parents have. I do want him, though, to live a sight better!" Jerusha Crone's tears, at this time, flowed easily. She did feel her own, and her husband's deficiency in force of Christian character, but she had not quite overcome her foolish application of the term "luck" to what superior character accomplished. It was still in a measure a blind to a full view of her Christian obligations. So, in God's kind providence, Patty and the Alden boys, supported by their parents, came in to supply to Tom the parental deficiency.

The winter school was again in operation. Mr. Everett had consented to become its teacher again, though offered better paying fields of labor. He was drawn to his former pupils by a strong friendship, increased by the religious interest among them. Patty's pupils were transferred to him, the Alden boys reciting their Latin and Greek privately, twice a week. He bore a generous testimony to the accuracy of their late teacher's instruction, as well as to the marked progress of the boys during the summer. But Patty retained her watchful care over the religious growth of the boys, especially of Tom.

There was quite an unpleasant feeling in the family of Joel Organ during the week before the commencement of the school. "Mary," said Joel to his wife, "I am determined that Fred shall go to school this winter, in spite of your nervous fear that our secret will get out."

"Fear!" retorted Mary, sharply. "You needn't accuse me of being afraid of the Crones, nor anybody who pretends to be their friend. But it's for the *boy's* good that I would have our secret kept."

"The boy's good!" replied Mr. Organ, sneeringly.

This remark wounded Mrs. Organ, and she replied, smartly, "You men folks do so *ache* to tell all you know!"

Joel left the house in anger, slamming the door as he retired. He found Fred in the barn, whom he addressed in a tone in nowise fitted to soothe his perplexed and burdened feelings. "Fred!" said the father.

"What sir?" answered Fred, startled by the excited voice and manner of his father.

"Fred!" repeated Joel, "do you go to school on Monday. And if you tell any person our secret, I'll skin you!"

Fred began to cry. "All the boys," he sobbed, "will be teasing me, and I don't want to go to school!"

"Well," replied his father, in a softened tone, "you can keep your mouth shut about it, can't you?"

"Don't know, sir," replied Fred.

"If you *do* tell!" said his father, again roused to fury, as he shook his fist in the face of his boy.

When Mr. Organ told his wife that he had "decided" that Fred should attend school, there was another scene, which ended in a violent fit of crying by Mrs. Organ. Her husband soothed her feelings in his way, by reminding her that she "didn't care who knew the secret. Not she! It was nothing *she* was ashamed of!"

Fred did attend the school on Monday. His bearing was that of the Crone boys a year before, but not that of Thomas Crone now. When the first week closed, and Saturday night closed, Fred and his parents were sitting by the kitchen fire. But little had been said during the week of the "teasing" of the boys. He had grown more cheerful after each day's attendance at school, and now his good spirits appeared in his face. He has rid himself of our vexatious secret, thought his father, and feels better for it; and I don't care if he has, for it must come out some time. His wife did not dare to ask Fred, for she dreaded the consequences to him and herself of any course he might take. At length Fred broke the painful silence. "Mother!" he exclaimed, "*all* the boys at school are real kind. They are as good again as they were last winter!"

"And coaxed out of you all you know, I'll warrant!" said his mother, waiting with an anxious face for his reply.

"No, they have never teased nor coaxed me about our secret," said Fred, cheerfully. "I guess they have forgotten all about that." A pause followed, which Fred broke by saying, in a low, thoughtful tone, "I don't know though as they have." He was thinking of Thomas Crone's care-worn look, although he did seem so much smarter, and better behaved than he did a year before.

Fred continued to report the kind bearing of all the school, and the especial attention of the Alden boys, and the "real good sort of way" of "Tom Crone." "Why, mother," said Fred, "Tom is getting real smart, and he seems to love me better than he loves any of the boys!"

"Coaxing round you?" said his mother, inquiringly.

"I'd like to know what reason Tom's got to coax round our Fred!" interposed Mr. Organ."

This remark shut off further talk. But an impression had been made upon the parents of which they were not yet ready to speak. Indeed, they did not know what either to think or say of the changed spirit at school. But it led them to venture to go to town to church, which they had not done for many months. The result was a greater perplexity than ever. Every one was kind and attentive. Even the Crones, Ezekiel and his wife, approached them with a cordiality which they could not, or rather, as it was in the presence of others, dared not repel. They went home, pondering upon the altered spirit of the people of the town. Their visits at the church became constant, when the winter storms did not prevent. While this feeling of interest is growing in the Organ family, we will note more fully the cause which so puzzled them.

"Thomas," said Patty, as he was about to commence study in the winter school, "you must *work* for the Saviour this winter." Thomas hung his head despondingly. Patty had often, in general terms, spoken to her young friends to learn early an *active* piety, but she had never put the duty home so directly to him.

"What can I do?" was the timid reply.

"If any boy has ever injured you, watch for an opportunity to do him a favor; that will be *one* way to begin to do something to show your love for Christ," replied Patty, with animation.

Thomas was much impressed with this remark. When he was sitting by the great fire-place of the kitchen that evening, around which the whole family were gathered, and *felt* the change — the pleasant change which had come over the spirit of his home, the remark of Patty came to him with new force. "There's Fred," he mused. "If anybody has injured me it is he. Wonder if he will be at school this winter?" So when these two boys met, a surprise of which we know something was prepared for Fred. Thomas Crone, owing to his summer study, was now among Mr. Everett's best scholars. The reproach of Crone's Corner was fading out. Energy, industry, and good character were slowly but surely bringing "good luck." So Fred was glad to receive Tom's special attentions, and occasional aid in his studies.

At Alden Farm bolder efforts were planned to win the Organs into the pleasant, though narrow paths of true wisdom. While the boys were throwing the silken cords of a Christian love around Fred, their parents were praying for and watching a favoring opportunity to speak to Joel and Mary Organ. The increasing interest of the Organs in the service of the house of worship encouraged these efforts.

"Patience," said John Alden, on Sabbath evening, after a most joyous day in the courts of the Lord; "Patience, we must go and make Joel and Mary Organ a call. I seem drawn towards them."

"They seem much drawn towards the people of God and His house," remarked Patience.

Carver, who had heard this remark, whispered to Miles, "Miles, I wish *we* could go to Fred Organ's. I guess he would be glad to see us."

"He *is* a different boy from what he was last winter," said Miles.

But John and Patience chose to make the call first alone, which they did, arriving early on a clear, moonlight evening. The level snow had made fine sleighing. The shrubbery along the road sparkled with pearly icicles, and the clear, cold air echoed to the merry bells. Even John Alden's horse seemed inspired by the errand of Christian love of those he bore, for, though he had seen fifteen winters, Patience declared that he "skipped over the road like a colt."

The visitors were received cordially. Earlier in the winter, Mary Organ's face would have been flushed with suspicion and ill-will towards such callers. But she had been disarmed, as much through the treatment of Fred as by courtesies to herself. No allusion was made to the Crones, and the heart of Mrs. Organ was open to the influence of faithful Christian labor to win her to Christ. Her husband was even more within such an influence. As to Fred, though addressed by a few words only, the words and spirit of the visitors fell upon his heart as light and heat upon the opening flower. So swiftly did the moments fly, that even the Aldens were beguiled into a later hour than usual. Nor was the pleasure of the occasion aided by even an offer of wine from the sideboard, nor cider from the cellar. Joel had plenty of both, and to most other callers they would have been tendered as a necessary politeness. But John Alden's emphatic "*No, sir*," was known as far as his face or name was recognized. When prayer was offered by Mr. Alden, it melted all hearts by its tender, earnest simplicity and directness. He means *me* by every word of his prayer, thought Mrs. Organ. He asks a blessing for *you*, whispered the Spirit in the heart of Mr. Organ. Fred wiped his eyes when the prayer closed, and was truly thankful that the whole of it had been for *him*.

When the visitors had gone, the Organ family sat for some moments around their blazing fire in silence. Though no angels unawares had been entertained, but only the renewed of the earthly church, a heavenly influence seemed to linger about the room.

"Mary," said Mr. Organ, breaking the silence, "have we any better friends than John and Patience?"

"None," answered his wife.

Another pause followed, which Fred interrupted, by saying, timidly, "I haven't any better friends than Carver, Miles, and —"

He hesitated to add the name he intended, and looked into his mother's face for permission.

"And who, Fred?" said his mother, in a tone which intimated her willingness to hear even *the* hated name.

"And Tom Crone," said Fred, with a choked utterance.

Silence again reigned, but no look evidenced displeasure at the declaration.

"And we are concealing in our own burdened hearts a fact which would rejoice the heart of each of them," said Mr. Organ, feelingly. Mrs. Organ buried her face in her hands and began a subdued sobbing, which she tried in vain to suppress. There was a severe conflict going on in her mind between a newly awakened sense of duty, and a long cherished pride and resentment. She began to see that to have peace within, to which she had long been a stranger, she must humble herself before both God and man. Her husband had less pride and regard for what others might think or say in reference to a line of conduct which for about a year had been a secret in the family, but he had a strong will, perversely set in the wrong direction. "I won't," struggled violently in his breast, with the Holy Spirit inspired duty of saying,—

> "Nay, but I yield, I yield,
> I can hold out no more;
> I sink, by dying love compelled,
> And own Christ conqueror."

Fred looked into the face of one parent

and then of the other. He perceived, with joy, in their flushed expression, not the old anger, but an anxious concern. He knew, too, what it meant. He had himself felt it deeply and bitterly. But his contact with better spirits at school, and his more susceptible, youthful feeling, had caused already the yielding. He longed for the permission of his parents to tell the Crones and his Alden friends all he knew concerning the missing boy, and to confess his own part in the guilty transaction. He felt that it would be a luxury of joy to do so. It seemed to him the only bar to the peace which had for so many months been to him unknown. So Fred watched the increasing change in his parents with tearful interest. His mother, seeing his watchful eye ever upon her, said, with a harshness which only increased her own burden, "Fred, it's bed-time! Don't sit there staring at me!"

The boy retired immediately, but not

to sleep. His pillow was wet with his tears.

Mr. Organ walked the floor in silence for a while, his wife, at the same time, crying with great violence. Mr. Organ, growing impatient with his wife's tears and sobs, said, rather sharply, "Mary, what's the use of all this ado! If we *must* tell what we have done, let us do it and be done with it!"

"Joel, I wish you'd go to bed and let me alone!" replied his wife, looking up through her tears and disheveled hair, the victim still of a hateful passion, that the reproving Spirit would displace for one of penitence, confession, love, and the peace that passes understanding.

Joel retired to his chamber, where the struggle in his breast went on for some time, when he fell asleep. With Mrs. Organ there was no sleep. Her bitterness towards her family had aggravated her sorrow, and for hours the storm within raged furiously. "O my God, *can* such a wretch be forgiven!" she at last exclaimed, aloud.

The stillness of the midnight hour gave impressiveness to the utterance. She became more calm, and prayed more deliberately, "Blessed Saviour, pardon my sin! It's dreadful black! Forgive! Oh, do forgive me!" The calm increased. She took the Word of God, dusty and long neglected, and sat down at the stand and spread it out before her. She opened it at the narrative of the crucifixion of Jesus. She read, with an interest she had never before felt, the moving story. When she read, "Father, forgive them for they know not what they do," she laid her forehead upon the open page and wept anew. Her tears were not now rebellious and bitter, but penitent and tender. The duty of confession did not seem so difficult as it had done a few hours before. The willingness to do so, as it came stealing in upon her heart, lifted in a measure her burden. She fell upon her knees and began her confession to him whom she had most offended — Jesus, the Lord and Saviour.

When Joel Organ came down from his sleeping-room, a little earlier than common, the breakfast was ready to go on the table. The kitchen glowed with a cheerful warmth, and a serious but pleasant glow rested upon the face of his Mary. "Joel," she said, with a soft, firm voice, "I have made up my mind what to do."

"So have I," said Joel, biting his lips to keep from breaking down into a cry as violent as that in which his wife indulged the night before.

"I mean," continued Mrs. Organ, "to go this very night and tell John and Patience — all about it!"

"That is what I want to do," said her husband. "It will be easier to confess to Ezekiel and Jerusha, after that."

A slight shadow passed over his wife's

face at the allusion to the severest test of her penitence. But it was momentary. With recovered self-possession, she said, firmly, "Yes, I know John will go with us, and encourage us in the duty."

CHAPTER XVIII.

THE COMFORTER.

The family at Alden Farm were not surprised at seeing the sleigh of Joel Organ drive into their yard. The penetrating eyes of John and Patience, saw that a burden was resting upon their friends' hearts too heavy to be long borne. They suspected too, the cause of that burden. But they wisely left them to the strivings of Him whose office-work it is to awaken and renew. Fervent and constant prayer was being offered by many for them. Ezekiel Crone and his wife were greatly encouraged concerning their conversion when they saw their renewed attention to the preached Word; and when they heard of John's and Patience's visit,' they became exceeding joyful. Mrs. Crone's customary expression was immediately upon her lips. "Ezekiel!" she exclaimed, "John and Patience have got hold of our Joel and Mary. He's bound to have good luck with them. He always does, you know. If you and I had gone to their house, the old mad would have shown itself in them right off. But now something will be done." Mrs. Crone dropped her voice into a low, tremulous tone, as she added, "Maybe John will get them to tell if they know anything about our Zeke. I am sure if they really mean to be Christians, they'll confess all."

"That they will," replied Mr. Crone, wiping the tear from his face; "and if they can bring Zeke back to us again, we'll all confess."

Mrs. Crone's heart responded to this last remark. So the line of duty which had been undertaken by the Aldens, in their evening's ride, was likely to be attended by rich fruit.

Scarcely were Joel and Mary seated by the evening lamp of their friends, when Mrs. Organ exclaimed, as she burst into tears, "We know where Zeke is! We helped him off! Can anybody ever forgive us!"

"It was a mean act in us!" exclaimed Joel, as he rose from his chair in his excitement, and walked the floor. "And a wicked thing, as I view it now," he continued, rubbing his hands and quickening his steps. Then, a few moments after, stopping directly in front of Mr. Alden's chair, and looking him full in the face, he asked, earnestly, "Do you think God can forgive such mean wickedness?"

"He has forgiven *me*," said Mr. Alden, fervently.

"*You! you!* John, who never did anything but good all the days of your life! such as you"—

"Hush! Joel," said Mr. Alden, rising and laying his hand gently on his friend's shoulder, while his lip quivered with emotion, "hush, Joel, the Spirit will be grieved by such talk. You know not what you say! Jesus, our Lord and Saviour, raised the dead when he gave *me* a new life! Say, 'This is a faithful saying and worthy of all acceptation, that Christ Jesus came into the world to save sinners, of whom I am chief.'"

"Yes, I *am* the chief of sinners," replied Joel. "I stole a son away from his parents. I have wickedly concealed the fact, and tried to justify it by many foolish and wicked arguments constantly preached to myself. *Can I be forgiven?*"

"I have been much worse than you, Joel," interposed his wife. "You'd never sent Zeke away if it hadn't been for me, and you would have brought him back long ago if *I* had not persisted in keeping up the lying to him and others. *I* am the greatest sinner."

A gleam of joy shot across the face of Patience Alden, at this unusual spirit of contention. "When the Spirit lifts the vail from a sinner's heart, he sees his own sins as the greatest," she said, softly.

John Alden's words were few, but they were spoken by divine help, and went directly to the hearts of the inquirers. They then kneeled together before God. John Alden had learned, as he said, to turn all the sin-sick who came inquiring of him, over to the Great Healer. He often sung,—

>"None but Jesus
>Can do helpless sinners good."

So he made short work of their case by bringing them to the Master. It seemed to the penitents that a divine voice spoke in every word of the prayer. It spoke not in wrath, for they had "not come to the mount that might be touched, and that burned with fire, nor unto blackness, and darkness, and tempest, and the sound of a trumpet, and the voice of words;" * * * "but to Jesus the Mediator of the new covenant, and to the blood of sprinkling, that speaketh better things than that of Abel." So their tears were dried; their burdens were removed; their darkness disappeared, and the true light of the believer came pouring into their minds and hearts.

"John, will you accompany us to Ezekiel Crone's?"

"To-night, Joel?" said Mr. Alden, smiling.

"Yes, to-night. I now feel just like going."

"Patience, you will go too?" inquired Mrs. Organ.

Mr. and Mrs. Alden were not reluctant to comply with the request. Though it would be a late hour to make a call, the work to be done was that of Christian duty, which promised the special blessing of the Saviour upon all concerned.

"Jerusha will bitterly reproach me for my part in getting Zeke off," thought Mrs. Organ, as she mused in silence while they rode to Crone's Corner. "Well," she submissively responded to the thought, "let her reproach me, I deserve it. She cannot say too hard things about me. I will hear it all, and tell her I shall despise myself for it as long as I live."

Joel Organ mused thus: "Ezekiel Crone knows I have greatly wronged him; and *I* know it. Ezekiel can say hard things when he gets roused, and if anything ever gave him a good reason to be roused, my treatment of his family has. So Ezekiel will attack me fiercely with his tongue, and before John and Patience too. Well, I'll let him. It will be good enough for me; and when he is done, I'll tell him if he will forgive me, I'll be his best friend."

With these feelings the party arrived at the Corner. The dog announced their coming by loud barking.

"Who can be coming at this late hour?" said Mr. Crone, laying down his book, in which he had been deeply interested. Thomas, who had been quite absorbed in his school lesson, ran to the door to call the dog away from the strangers. "It's John Alden's sleigh, I know it by the bells!" he exclaimed, stepping back to get his cap.

"And the sleigh too of our Joel and Mary, as you live!" exclaimed Mrs. Crone, with a flush of delight, placing a candle in the window to light them up the path, and going to the door to meet them. Mr. Crone and Tom had shouted their hearty welcome when the visiting party had hardly moved to leave the sleigh. Mrs. Crone greeted them cordially in the entry, throwing her arms about Mrs. Organ's neck and kissing her, while both wept freely.

"You will loathe me!" sobbed Mrs. Organ, "when you know how mean and wicked

I have been. I sent Zeke off, and kept him away."

"It's enough! My boy will return then!" said Mrs. Crone, kissing her visitor again as she drew a chair for her, and began at the same time to aid in removing her "muff and tippet," and heavy over-clothes. The meeting of the men was with more self-control. "I am glad to see you, Joel," Mr. Crone repeated, as he took his hat and heavy overcoat. "Thank you!" said Mr. Organ, with a desperate effort to keep calm. The Aldens divided the attention of the rest of the company for a while, and all sat down around the blazing fire.

"Ezekiel," said Mr. Organ, directing his attention to Mr. Crone, "your whole year of suffering for the loss of your boy is owing to me; getting and keeping him away is all my wicked work."

"Joel, say more mine," interposed his wife, breaking down again with the rush of uncontrollable emotion.

Joel paused for a moment, awaiting the scourging of Ezekiel's tongue, which he knew so well how to lay on, and which Joel had so keenly felt aforetimes.

"Joel, it was all of God," replied Mr. Crone, with a Christian composure, which amazed his relatives. "We needed such a correction of our great faults as parents."

"That we did!" interposed Mrs. Crone. "We have been greatly to blame about Zeke. Joel and Mary needn't think any thing more about it. Only let us have Zeke back again, and we will be loving friends."

"There, now, this is what Christ can do when he gets in the heart," said Mr. Alden. "Friends, let us sing, 'All hail the power of Jesus' name!'" The hymn was sung as it never was before at Crone's Corner. Jerusha and Mary kneeled at the same chair, when Mr. Alden offered the sacrifice of praise, and made supplication for continued grace. Their arms were thrown over each other in loving embrace, and God's blessing sealed their secret vow of perpetual reconciliation.

When Joel and Mary arrived at their own home, they found Fred waiting with deep interest. "My son," said his mother, with great animation, "you have kept everything looking nicely. It was never so pleasant here before." The result of the visit was already told, and Fred's heart leaped for joy. He read the good news in the faces of both parents. He would be compelled no longer to carry the burdensome secret on his own heart. He hastened to school the next morning by the way of Crone's Corner. He had already made the confession to God of the wrong of his own part in the guilty affair, and he longed for the opportunity to confess it to Tom and his parents. But the injured ones anticipated his coming with joy, and greeted him with the words of forgiving love.

"Zeke Crone is found and is coming home!" were words upon every tongue the following morning. The news flew about the town, like the news of peace after the long, dark night of war. "I hope his father will flog him well!" exclaimed a gruff old lounger at the tavern bar, who had come for his morning dram.

"Old Zeke Crone will know how to lay it on," replied the bar-keeper, filling up his customer's glass.

"Yes, and Zeke will know how to give it to them Organs too," replied old Gruff, holding for a moment the glass to his lips.

A few only of the school children were disposed to taunt Fred with what had occurred. Tom's loving intimacy with him, and the genuine undisguised friendship of the Aldens, Carver and Miles, did much to shield him. Besides, his own tears, when the subject was alluded to, were of themselves a good defense and the best apology for his wrong to all the right minded.

CHAPTER XIX.

THE DECEIVERS AND THE DECEIVED.

Since Joel Organ and his wife, followed by Fred, have told their secret concerning Zeke, we are afforded an opportunity to give the history of his years from home.

On that night when the uproar in the Crone kitchen drove him in a tempest of passion out of the house, he had no settled purpose of action. There was that desperation of feeling impelling his hurried steps over the parental threshold, which often pushes youth, in a moment of frenzy, beyond the bounds of restraint, into outbreaking sin. Zeke stood for a few moments in the woodshed, a volcano of passion. Before reason had resumed her throne, he thought he heard the steps of his father approaching the door. He rushed from the shed, out of the yard into the street, and down the road leading towards the Organ farm. He had then no intention of going there. He found relief in running, and so he ran until out of breath. He then paused, turned round and listened. He thought he heard the faint sound of his father in pursuit, though it was but the echo of his own panting breath. He started again, and hurried forward until he had reached the neighborhood of his hating and hated relatives. When his now slow and hesitating step had brought him to the gate of Joel Organ's house, reason began its unequal contest with passion. "I'll go in, and tell Joel and Mary how they abuse me at home," he muttered, spitefully. "But Joel will abuse me again and turn me out doors," was suggested to himself. "If he does, and won't care where I go nor what I do, I won't care if I freeze to death. I wish I was dead!"

The cold wind was blowing a piercing breeze upon the unhappy boy. The perspiration produced by his run was fast subsiding into a violent chill. The world, it seemed to him, had turned against him, and wherever he turned, he was confronted with misery. He was about to exclaim, "I don't care! I wish I was dead!" when the imploring, loving countenance of Carver, as he threw himself between the rod of the teacher and Zeke's back, came before him. He seemed to hear again his voice, saying, "Don't strike him, sir! Please, Mr. Everett, don't strike Zeke, he isn't to blame!" It was the coming and whispering of the good angel, to save from utter ruin the imperiled heart. Passion gave way to reason, and Zeke whispered, "I'll go in, and stay awhile and warm me, and then go home." The dog, as Zeke approached the house, made a noisy outcry, which brought Joel to the door. Zeke rushed in, and was fairly in the house before he was recognized. His countenance and shivering limbs spoke for him, and touched even Mary Organ's heart. She immediately set to work to make him comfortable, talking the while most bitterly against the home and its inmates which he had just left. "It's no more than I should have expected!" she exclaimed. "It's just like your father and mother. I have known them always. Turning their child out-door in mid-winter to freeze to death! That's a pretty kind of business for Christians! If that's religion, I don't want any of it!" Having thus spoken her mind of the parents, she turned to the boy with words of affected sympathy. "You've stood it, Zeke, longer than I would if I'd been you. You're a fool if you ever go back!"

"Ever go back!" were words which startled Zeke. He had not thought of not returning. In fact, he had been *drifting* before a tempest of passion, but now that reason was getting her hand upon the helm, he would have started back to the port from which he came. To prevent this, Mrs. Organ kept a breeze in motion in another direction. She placed the boy on the great settle before the fire, drew off his boots and stockings, and rubbed his feet and hands; she then brought water to wash his soiled face; and finally, set before him a warm, inviting supper. He had eaten but little since the morning, and the food relished well. Mrs. Organ sat down beside him, and assuming a tender tone, such as was well suited to his wounded feelings, she said, "Ezekiel, I *do* pity you. You will never be anything while you stay at home; you *know* you won't. Nobody could be. You are not a mite to blame for not getting along well in school."

"I don't think I am," interposed Zeke, with feeling.

"No," continued Mrs. Organ, "you are

not. No one thinks you are. Now, if I was you, I would go off where I could live in peace, and by and by, when your folks get sorry for their bad treatment, you can come back, and show them that you can take care of yourself. It will make a man of you, Zeke, to go away and set up for yourself."

Zeke's resentment was still hot enough, and his wounded feelings tender enough, to lead him to listen to this wicked counsel. To deepen his wrong purposes, Mr. Organ put in his bad words just here.

"No boy of your spirit," he exclaimed, in a rough way, "will submit to what you have to. Besides, Zeke, your folks will be glad to get rid of you; so will all the people of the town."

This last declaration was spoken with intense bitterness. It was the unkindest cut of all. Zeke made no answer, and soon retired to bed with angry passions at fever heat. Sleep departed from his eyes, so that while his burdened parents and sorrowing brother were watching out the weary hours at the old home, he was full of tossing and tears.

"Glad to get rid of me!" he continually repeated to himself. "Glad to get rid of me! Well, I guess I will show them that I can take care of myself. I *won't* go back. I'll die first!"

In his heart, he did not stop to inquire whether Joel had spoken the truth. Angry passion is both blind and deaf. It plunges into the surging sea first, and then when helplessly struggling with its waves, considers how escape can be made possible.

"Joel," said Mrs. Organ, "we've got a chance at last to pay off the grudge we owe the Crones. They've turned up their noses at us long enough. We'll pay them off well!"

"We'll plague them," echoed Mr. Organ.

"Do you go to town to-morrow, and when you come back tell Zeke that you have seen his folks, and that old Crone and his wife say that they hope they shan't hear from him this ten years, and that then they hope he will come back a decent man. Tell him, too, that his father says if he comes back before that time, he'll horsewhip him, and turn him out of door."

Joel Organ looked at his wife with astonishment. He was prepared for most any mean thing to spite the Crones, but this audacious lying surprised him. But he saw that his wife meant what she said, and he had learned to submit in such cases.

"But what shall we do with Zeke?" inquired Joel. "We don't want him hanging round here."

"Of course we don't, and won't have him neither," said Mrs. Organ, emphatically. "But I will manage that, if you will do as I say."

Joel smiled significantly and nodded assent.

"There's your old Uncle Prince," continued Mrs. Organ, "who lives up country. You know he said last fall, that he should want a boy before the spring opened. He's famous, you know, for taming wild colts and making bad boys toe the mark. Zeke will be a deal better off up there, and his absence for a month or two will do good at Crone's Corner. I will fix up some of Fred's old clothes for him, and do you write the old man Prince a letter for Zeke to take along with him. It will be a real blessing for all hands to have him go."

The next morning Joel Organ went about the business of carrying out his wife's plan, with a desperate sort of earnestness. He was off to town early, but not before Zeke was astir. The boy stood by the wagon as he was about to start, wavering in his resolution to separate himself from his home. Mrs. Organ's quick eye discerned this. Calling him into the house, she said, plausibly, "Mr. Organ is going to the town, and he will hear what they say at home about your absence. If they *desire* you to come back, and he can get any evidence that you won't be beat and turned out of doors, you can return. Otherwise, we will find a real good place for you."

With this assurance, Zeke willingly remained behind. But the day wore heavily away. He waited uneasily for Mr. Organ's return, for, though so deeply wounded, and so thoroughly excited to bad blood, there was a remaining longing for home — especially for re-union with Tom and the sisters.

"It's as I expected, Zeke," said Mr. Organ, as the homesick boy met him at the gate. "I saw good Deacon Turner to-day. The deacon's word, you know, can be relied upon. He said he had just been to the Corner, and that he was sorry to find your father and mother in such a wicked frame of mind. They declared, said the deacon, that their runaway boy should never come into the house again, or never, at least, until he had proved himself somewhere else a different boy. Your father declared that if you did come, he would horsewhip you and turn you out again. And the deacon further said that even Tom and the young sisters seemed well satisfied to have their brother gone, and he guessed they would be quite as well off without Zeke, and he hoped it would be best for Zeke himself." Mr. Organ added to these lying words the remark that he had not told any one that he knew anything about the runaway, and as people didn't seem to care what had become of him, he had no difficulty in keeping the secret.

Zeke's heart was full to breaking during this statement. When it was finished he cried outright. Mr. and Mrs. Organ scolded and ridiculed him by turns.

"There, Zeke," said Mrs. Organ, "I thought you had more spunk than that. I wouldn't be a baby. You see your folks don't care for you; why should you care? You can make a man of yourself yet, Zeke. Come, cheer up! I will fix you up a box of clothes this very day. We have got a good place all ready for you, where you'll have good treatment, better company, and a chance to study and read, so that by and by you can come back and show the people that Zeke Crone is somebody."

"There, stop that blubbering!" exclaimed Mr. Organ, in a rough, unfeeling manner.

"Do show a little gumption," joined in Mrs. Organ.

But Zeke had his cry out. Grief was at length satisfied by the tears, and now resentment came in to give him a disposition to assent to, and even to join with some cordiality in the plans of his relatives. He began to believe what they so boldly assumed, that they were his best friends. He was kept closely in the house for two days, while Mrs. Organ mended and altered some old clothes, "running the heels" of a few pair of new stocking, and putting in, to make the rest more acceptable, a new overfrock, which, as Mrs. Organ remarked, was "as nice as a pink, and would do to wear to meeting."

Fred looked upon all these movements with mingled feelings. He hated, yet pitied Zeke. But his fear of his parents was his prevailing, daily experience. When he went to school he felt much the restraint in reference to betraying the secret he held, that a soldier feels when he fears to desert lest he be shot. So Zeke received only a cold kind of sympathy from Fred.

On the morning of the fourth day of his departure from home, long before the tardy winter sunrising sparkled on the snowy hilltops, Joel Organ and Zeke were on their way to the "Eagle Tavern," twenty-five miles distant. The sleighing was excellent. The "turning out" was the only impediment to their rapid progress, for the heavy sleds carrying wood and logs had done most of the breaking out, so that the snow wall on either side was hard and steep. But at this early hour, but few teams were met. Mrs. Organ had put Zeke on a stool in the bottom of the sleigh, and covered him up with a heavy blanket. "Now, Zeke," she said, emphatically, affecting a tender interest in him, "you will freeze if you show your head outside of the blanket. You may *peek out*, that's all."

Joel gave his wife a knowing wink, as much as to say, *I* understand, and drove off. He was well out of the vicinity of all who might recognize him, before he allowed Zeke to sit on the seat, and look out upon the country they were passing.

It was yet scarcely the early dinner hour when our travelers arrived at the Eagle Tavern. It was on the stage road to the country home of Capt. James Prince, yet fifty miles away. Joel drove under the horse-sheds, took out the baiting he had brought with him, and fed his horse, and then sat in the sleigh and ate the lunch which his wife had carefully stowed away under the seat. There was enough to eat, and that which was good, but Zeke relished nothing, though urged to help himself. Their drink was a small can of cold coffee, whose lack of warmth was made up by a bottle of rum and molasses, of which both took a sip. Joel despised drunkards, and took his moderate sip of rum every day. He had kept far away from the influence of John Alden's "temperance notions," and so was in the darkness of heathenism as to *true* temperance. The luck of Alden Farm in possessing light on this subject, had thrown some rays into Zeke's mind. So he took the poisonous sip reluctantly, and with some forbiddings of conscience. But his will in this direction was not up to the "*no*" point, and he yielded to Joel's gruff, "It will do you good, boy."

Mr. Organ now went into the tavern, sat down by the bar-room fire, chatted with the loungers, answered all their questions as to where he came from, what he was there for, where the boy was going, and on to the end of the asking, as readily as a stranger in our modern cars tells the conductor at what depot he wishes to get off. He then introduced the case of Zeke to the barteuder, had his name, town to which he was to go, and person, Captain James Prince, to whom he was consigned, booked, and paid his fare and night's lodging. This official — the bar-tender — agreed to see Zeke on the stage in due season, the next morning, and give the driver the proper orders for his delivery. This done, Joel turned to Zeke, slipped into his hand, with an air of one doing a deed of becoming generosity, a Spanish "quarter" for contingencies by the way, and said, striking him familiarly on the back, "Good luck to you, Zeke," entered his sleigh and drove homeward.

Zeke had been entrusted with his box of clothes,—which the bar-tender put among the baggage for the morning stage,—and with his box of provisions for board. Besides, Mr. Organ had given him a sealed letter of introduction to his Uncle Prince. It read as follows:

"DEAR UNCLE:—Knowing that you want a boy for all-work about the house and farm, I send you Ezekiel Crone. His parents have cruelly turned him out-doors. He is rather a bad boy, but under your hand I have no doubt he will render you good service.

"Your Nephew,
"JOEL ORGAN."

Zeke was thus starting in the world for

himself. Wronged at home by blundering parents; wronged by those who affected to be his friends, by placing him in a false position towards his parents; and to be disparaged in the eyes of those to whom he was going, by the very announcement of his coming; and, worst of all, having but little knowledge of the right way, and loving it less. But there was One whose eye was upon the wandering boy; "whose compassions fail not," and whose "mercy is higher than the heavens"; who saw the tears which were shed for him, in spite of the lying of his professed friends; who heard the prayers at the Corner, at the Alden Farm, and from many other devout hearts;—One, whose blessings are life and peace.

Zeke remained in the bar-room, listening to the talk of the loungers, seeing the smoking and drinking, hearing the profanity, until the sights and sounds sickened his mind and heart. He looked into the village store, but it was only a little different in its atmosphere and company, from the tavern. He walked through the village to the side on which stood the church and school-house. The scholars were just coming out with a shout and running towards their home. Zeke wiped a tear from his eye, which was soon dry as he recalled Joel's declaration, "They are glad to get rid of you at home!" He returned to the bar-room, ate his supper by the fire, drank a few cents' worth of rum and molasses, and went early to bed, with a feeling of reckless disregard of the future.

CHAPTER XX.

LONELY AND COMFORTLESS.

It was just as the night was coming on, when Zeke was left at the house of Captain James Prince. His box was tossed after him by the unceremonious stage-driver, who exclaimed, "Here, boy, this is the place where you are to stop; now behave yourself or "— Zeke lost the last sentence, as the driver mounted the stage box, gave his whip a crack and dashed away. He walked up to the front door, letter in hand, and lifted the heavy knocker; the noise, as it rung through the house, struck also to the homesick boy's heart. The captain himself came to the door. He was a tall, well-proportioned, strong, rough, but not to those who knew him, an unkind looking man. He was well-dressed in a farmer's home-spun suit. He wore spectacles, and looked over the top of them at the stranger-boy, with his large, piercing eyes. If he had been the Czar of all the Russias he would not have more awestruck him as he handed the letter. The captain read it, crushed it in his great brawny hand, took off his glasses, and looked at him for a few moments in silence. They seemed to Zeke snail-creeping moments. "You should have gone to the side door, boy," he said, at length, in a decided tone. Zeke stood statue-like, not knowing whether he should now go to the side door, or come in at that where the master of the house stood, or go away altogether, and have the door shut in his face. Captain Prince saw his confusion, and said, in a softer tone, "Well, never mind, now. Come along." Zeke followed through the parlor, through the sitting-room, where Mrs. Prince was sitting, into the kitchen. "There — let me see, what is your name?" said the captain, smoothing out the letter and adjusting his spectacles. "Ezekiel, sir; they call me Zeke."

"Ezekiel never should be called Zeke," said the captain, sharply. "I never will allow it in my house. There, Ezekiel, sit down on the settle!"

Captain Prince returned to the sitting-room without saying another word.

"Pray, husband, who have you there?" said Mrs. Prince. Her husband read the letter, and neither said a word for some minutes. "Do you wish, husband, a boy who has been turned out-door by his parents?" suggested Mrs. Prince.

"Don't know; some parents are indiscreet," replied the captain, with a dignity, which, to a stranger, would have seemed haughty.

"But Joel says he is rather a bad boy," remarked Mrs. Prince.

"He may not remain so," replied the captain, resuming the examination of the papers in which he had been engaged. Mrs. Prince arose and went into the kitchen. She cast a momentary glance at Zeke, but it seemed to him that she read his thoughts and knew his whole history. The only other persons in the kitchen were an ancient maiden, whom they called Nancy, and John, the hired man. Neither of these important personages had appeared to take the least notice of the boy. John was reading, and was evidently profoundly indifferent to his case, whether he stayed or left. Nancy had grown up from early womanhood in the family as help. She disliked children, and was fond of saying that she was "glad and thankful" that there had never been "a screaming young one" in the family. Young people she barely endured, especially boys. She would "fidget" immediately if one came to the house, and walked with soiled feet across her spotless white floor. She hoped that Zeke was only a passer-by, whom the captain had admitted to spend a few moments at the fire.

"Nancy, get this boy, Ezekiel, some supper, and then conduct him to the boy's room, where he will sleep. John, bring his box from the side of the road, where I saw the stage-man drop it. Ezekiel, wash your face and hands before eating, for I see they are soiled by your travel, and then wash them again after supper. There is the sink, and yonder is the 'roller.' The time here for boys to retire is half-past eight, in the winter. You see the clock in the corner of the kitchen."

All these orders were uttered in a matter-of-course way, and obeyed, so far as John and Nancy were concerned, as a matter of course. Nancy felt fidgety at his introduction into the family. But then, what of that! She understood that it was simply none of her business, which was a short way, at least, of settling the matter. Ezekiel ate his supper, and, in spite of many strange emotions, he ate heartily. He had not eaten a warm meal since leaving Joel's, and Nancy's toast, warmed-over hashed meat, and cup of tea, were relished well. Having finished supper, he went back to his place near the fire, watching the while the clock for the hand to approach eight and a half. When eight o'clock was noted on the dial plate, he arose, saying, "I think I won't wait until half past eight, I'm tired," intimating to Nancy his desire to be shown to his room. Nancy kept on sewing, and the boy stood in the floor looking at her with a puzzled air. He was at a loss to know what next to say or do.

Nancy looked at him a moment, and said, curtly, "Better wash your face and hands; as the mistress bid you, and not be soiling my clean sheets the first thing."

The words struck Zeke like a current of electricity. "I don't want you to wipe all the dirt off your hands on my clean roller, neither; wash them clean," added Nancy, without raising her eyes from her work. Seeing this condition fulfilled, she took the light and bid Ezekiel follow her. She led the way to a room over the wood-shed, next to John's. It looked inviting, however; a piece of domestic matting spread before the bed, a stand placed under a small glass, and a chair, with the bed and its clean sheets, completed the furnishing. "Remember that four o'clock is the time to get up," said Nancy, setting down the lamp and disappearing without wasting breath on any ceremonious "I hope you'll like your new quarters," or, "May you sleep well," or even a "Good night."

"Seems to me," muttered Zeke, "these folks are amazing short; how shall I know when it's four o'clock!" Tired and homesick, yet irritated and discouraged by the past, and reckless of the future, he fell asleep.

Captain James Prince was a retired shipmaster. Having made a number of successful voyages, and amassed some wealth, to which his wife had, later in life added still greater by inheritance, he had come back to the home of his youth, thinking to find retirement and agreeable rest in farming. He had found the retirement, but not the rest. He was as restless as the ocean on whose bosom he had sailed. He had altered everything about the old homestead, much to the disgust of all the surviving friends in the town, of his father. He experimented with seeds, with the manner of planting and cultivating them, and with tools by which the work was done. He proved himself an experimenting but not an experienced farmer. The old cultivators of the soil shrugged their shoulders and grudged the money he wasted. He kept fine horses, and paid a high price for choice breeds of domestic animals. But, in spite of money spent, and scheming, of care, and no little real hard work — for the captain *could* lead off in hard work,— nothing resulted in gains which anything like approached the captain's idea of money-making. He was becoming disgusted, and more irritable than ever. He often walked his room, looked at the pictures of the ships which he had sailed, and threatened to go to sea again.

The captain never had any children, but he had taken many boys to bring up. His mode of managing his domestics and employees was that of the quarter-deck. Of conciliation, and the power of drawing others· after him by kindness, and a loving example, he knew nothing. But Captain Prince meant to be just. His word, everywhere, was as good as his note. If anything roused the profane anger of the old sailor more than flat disobedience in one under his authority, it was downright meanness. There was withal a tender place in the captain's heart, but some of his household thought that it was a long and bitter waiting before they found it.

Zeke did not wake up at four o'clock; of course he did not, for he was very tired, and his journey had been a wakeful one. The captain noticed it, and simply said, "Beware, boy, of the second time."

Zeke had wondered what there was to be done to require him to rise at four o'clock. But a sight of the long barn, and line of cattle to be cared for, including the milking of twenty cows, enlightened him. John had been at work two hours when Zeke made his appearance, and Nancy had the breakfast ready in the kitchen. The captain and his wife were astir, but took their breakfast later, in the dining-room. Nancy set the food before the new comer, but said nothing, and the whole meal was eaten without a word, except when something was wanted. John swallowed his food in haste, and returned to his work. "You'd better follow

John to the barn," said Nancy, before Zeke had swallowed the last mouthful. John pointed to the stalls of the horses, as much as to say, "You can well enough see what there is to be done. Do it." Zeke did know what was to be done, and, impelled by a fear he could not explain, but which burdened his spirits quite as much as it stimulated his hands, he worked with his full strength. He had cleaned out several stalls, and was driving at others, when, looking up, he saw the captain standing over him. His look did not express anger or reproof, but only inquiry. He was evidently satisfied for the moment with his new boy. He did not say so, though to have said, simply, "There! that's right, my boy!" or only, "Well done!" would have been so easy, cost so little, and done the little stranger's heart so much good. We have only this most miserable of all excuses for the captain: It was his way! If the boy had been loitering, or had done his work blunderingly, whew! how quick he would have opened his mouth, and how *sharp* the words would have been. Strange that with some people bitter complaints are thought to be worth more than rightful and timely commendations!

Zeke cleaned out all the stalls — a long, hard job, but one which had to be done every morning. Having done it, he said to himself, "I wonder where the bedding is? Nobody tells me anything." Stepping up to John, who was currying the carriage horse, he asked, "Will you tell, John, where the bedding is?"

"Use your eyes, boy, and find it," was the only reply, as John applied the currycomb with increased vigor, acting as if a word spoken was a moment lost. Ezekiel, in looking round, stumbled upon some fine hay which seemed to be lying about loosely. He began to pitch it into the stalls. "Hold on there, you booby! That's the feed of the young critters! Don't you know rowen from bedding!" The boy's face flushed with anger ⬛grief. He looked further through the ⬛connected sheds, and found, near the enclosures for the calves, some refuse hay and straw. This he ventured to pitch into the stalls. "That's more like it!" shouted John, in a softer tone, feeling some self-reproach for his harsh chidings. But he did not apologize for it. That would have been too truly manly for the spirit which pervaded the Prince farm.

When Zeke had completed his work on the stalls, he walked again along the front of each of them, feeling an honest self-approval for having done his work so well. John, who had looked through them all, thought the work well done, but seeing Zeke standing in a musing attitude, shouted, "Do you think, boy, you have done all there is to be done! Clear up the barn floor!"

Zeke started, at this rough demand, shocked as a boy on the track, in these days, would be at the sudden scream of a coming engine. "He needn't be so cross about it," muttered Zeke, going about the work immediately. "Everybody here is cross."

Thus sharply prompted, the stranger-boy went through his first day's work. The captain exchanged no words with him, except to give some order. When his supper was eaten, the chores being all done, he sat down on the great settle and looked into the fire. There were but few books in those days, and he had not learned to find instruction and amusement in them. It is so dull here, he mused, and he watched the clock for the welcome time of retiring. When it was eight o'clock, he could wait no longer. John and Nancy seldom spoke to one another, and never to him. He recollected, much to Nancy's satisfaction, to wash his face and hands before going to bed. There was no "good night" said, as he retired, for no one encouraged the kind expression. A certain indescribable fear burdened his mind, as he lay down, lest he should not awake at four o'clock. "Beware of the second time," rung in his ears, while the stern, overaweing face of the captain was ever before him, specter-like and distressing. Thus burdened he fell into an uneasy sleep. He had slept about two hours, when he started up in a fright. It must be late he thought. He hastily arose and began to dress himself. At that moment, he heard John in the entry. He opened the door and said, "Am I late, John? I will be down in a moment." "Guess you need not go down now. I'm just a-going to bed," replied John, gruffly. Zeke gladly returned to bed, and slept until John's heavy tread by his sleeping-room door awoke him. He soon followed him into the kitchen, where a roaring fire already made it look cheerful. "Can you milk?" inquired John.

"As well as anybody," replied Zeke, smartly. John smiled, but it was a cold, selfish kind of a smile, as he replied, "Well, boy, you may take that pail and follow me; you can have chance enough to show what you can do in that line." Zeke soon learned the truth of this. He was kept at work milking until his wrists ached, and he was glad to be relieved by the call to breakfast.

Thus working, watched by sharp eyes, and reproved with severity for every misstep, without any approving word, and with seldom a suggestion as to how his work should be done, Zeke passed the first six weeks. The spring had begun to displace the winter, and the work of the farm pressed more heavily than ever. He yearned for some one to talk to — for some vent to his pent up feelings. He began to spend his evenings in the grocery store, or in the bar-room of the neighboring tavern, listening to the idle gossip, and becoming familiar with their atmosphere of tobacco smoke, and to the low and profane talk of the half drunken men. The captain, whose watchfulness detected every movement of his domestics, cared nothing for this, so long as he was in bed at the assigned hour, eight and a half. He, of course, became more and more interested in the places and the company. There was in his heart the thought, nobody cares for me; and it shook the foundation of what little moral principle he had retained. One night the story-telling was unusually exciting, stimulated by a generous patronage of the bar. Zeke forgot the hour of returning home, until the bar-tender said, roughly, "Boy, you live with the captain, don't you?"

"Yes, sir," said Zeke, starting up.

"Well," said the liquor man, with a significant sneer, "It's ten o'clock, and he'll warm you up when you get home, or he an't Captain Jim Prince."

The dim light of the fire gleamed faintly in the kitchen, assuring Zeke as he looked through the window, that John and Nancy had gone to bed. I will slip in, he thought, and creep up to bed, and the captain will not know how long I was out. Opening the door softly, he drew off his heavy boots, warmed himself for a moment, and crept towards the stairway door. Suddenly, as a panther upon an unsuspecting deer, the captain, opening the door in the opposite side of the room, pounced upon him. Taking him by the collar, he lifted him easily from his feet, shook him violently, and then threw him his full length upon the floor. As he attempted to rise, the captain, with a sweep of his hand, laid him prostrate again. When he next ventured, a moment after, to stand upon his feet, he was alone. The captain had disappeared. No voice, nor sound, except that which had come from his violent handling, had Zeke heard. He went sobbing to bed, more crushed in heart than hurt in body. It was no comfort to him, in this state of mind, to hear, as he entered his room, a coarse, heartless laugh from John.

CHAPTER XXI.

THE ANGEL HELPER.

Zeke was at the morning work as soon as John, though he had slept but little. The captain was looking round as usual, but neither he, nor any one, alluded to the incidents of the evening before. Zeke now spent his evenings at home, which, of course, passed heavily away, as his chafed spirits were fast maturing into a readiness for almost any desperate act. But there was yet a tender recollection, to some extent, of those he had left far away. He thought of them in his silent musings at the evening fireside. He thought, with tender emotions, of the Alden boys, and especially of Carver, and of his last act of kindness at the school.

He would have written to his parents at once, and have thrown himself as a prodigal upon their forgiveness, but for Mr. Organ's assurance, "They are glad you are gone." How can the Aldens receive me, he reasoned, if my parents reject me. He would have even started on foot for home, begging his way from door to door, but for the ever-haunting thought, "They are glad you are gone." The letters which came occasionally from Joel and his wife, reported that everybody was satisfied with his absence. "The captain must recommend you after, at least, a year's trial," added Joel. "He will never say any good of me any way," muttered Zeke, on reading this statement. "It is only what he thinks is wrong that he can talk about. I don't care what becomes of me." Zeke began to seek his old haunts again, and even the fear of the captain restrained him but little. "A shaking up," and even a whipping, were defied. There was danger of his being kicked any day from the home of Captain Prince into the wide, friendless, wicked world, to drift more and more rapidly to utter moral ruin. But He who hears prayer, listened to the now humble and believing prayers offered in secret, and at the family altar at Crone's Corner. That watchful One cared for the oppressed and wronged, though sinning wanderer; *He* knew too what praying hearts at Alden Farm and Hope Cottage were offering loving supplications in his behalf. He had his own faithful ones even in the vicinity of the Prince farm, yet unknown to Zeke, whom He could send to bless with wise counsel and comforting sympathy, in answer to these prayers.

One night Zeke was, as usual, about to enter the tavern bar, when he felt the pressure of a soft hand on his shoulder. Looking around, his eyes met those of a Quaker lady of middle life. Her countenance, expressing great intelligence and heartfelt kindness, reminded him of that of Patience Alden. The tears at once started to his eyes, and he was completely under her control. "Ezekiel, thou should'st not enter there; it leadeth to death. Come with me, and I will do thee good." Ezekiel followed her at once. She led him to a cottage home near by. "Sit down, Ezekiel, and make thyself at home," said Aunt Huldah. Her name was Huldah Doane, but she was seldom referred to except as Aunt Huldah. "I have heard of thee often," she continued, "and learn that thee dost not do altogether right. But maybe thy sin is one of ignorance; if so, I desire, by the Spirit's help, to instruct thee. Don't thee wish, Ezekiel, to be instructed in the right way?"

"Yes, ma'am," said Zeke, feelingly.

"Wilt thee endeavor, by divine help, to keep in it?" asked Aunt Huldah, with pity and love beaming from every feature of her face, but in a voice more truly commanding than the thunder tones of Captain Prince. Zeke's only answer was a flood of tears. He had found a friend whose chiding even fell on his ear like the sweetest music. Though he knew it not, its tones were those for which his soul fainted.

"Thee need'st not speak, Ezekiel," said Aunt Huldah. "Thy tears are thy answer." Huldah's husband came in at this moment, whom she called Amos. He was more reserved in speech than his wife, but still his bearing toward the stranger-boy was that of real interest and kindness. Aunt Huldah said a few words concerning the evils of bad company, and invited Zeke to spend his leisure hours with her. "Thee canst sit by our stand, and read, when thee is not spoken to," said Huldah. "Should I have callers, my kitchen is equally pleasant, and thee canst quietly read. I have no child, and there is none to disturb thee." Huldah wiped an unforbidden tear from her eye as she said this. Her loved and only child, a son, died at ten years of age. He would, had he lived, been of Zeke's age.

"What is thy master's hour for thy returning?" inquired Huldah.

"At half past eight," replied Zeke.

"It is not quite that time," she replied, "but thee may'st go, so as to be sure of punctuality." It did not seem to Zeke twenty minutes since he passed her threshold, so swiftly had the time flown. "Be faithful to thy master," said Aunt Huldah, as Zeke passed out. "Do thy duty well, not with eye-service, as pleasing men; but as in the sight of God."

The work of the next day seemed lighter to Zeke than usual. The captain and the domestics noticed his special promptness in it, but they maintained the usual silence.

"Hast thee left no required work undone?" said Aunt Huldah, as Zeke entered at an early hour.

"No ma'am," said Zeke, honestly, for his lighter heart had made more thorough work at the farm.

"Then I bid thee welcome. Sit down, Ezekiel. Thee dost look weary. Amos has gone out on business, so we shall disturb no one by our talk. I will tell thee a tale of the olden times. It may rest thee."

Zeke thought he was never so little tired in his life. Huldah's loving words sent his blood coursing with invigorating swiftness through his veins. Huldah worked away, telling her story of the sufferings for conscience sake, of one of her own religious faith, relieving the seriousness of the story by a quiet humor for which she was remarkable.

"It's eight o'clock, Ezekiel," said Aunt Huldah, bringing her story to a sudden end.

"It's too bad," said Zeke, "to have to go now. I don't see why the captain cannot let me stay until nine. That is early enough to go home."

"Thee may'st not be the best judge," said Aunt Huldah, chidingly. "Thee should'st obey without gainsaying." Zeke felt the kind reproof, and retired promptly.

The captain noticed the change for the better in Zeke. He learned, too, that he was not now seen at the gatherings of the idlers at the store or bar-room, but did not at once learn what other place of resort he had found. He was satisfied that he had found better company, so he made no inquiry. When, after several weeks, he learned that he had become intimate at Amos Doane's, and was under the training of his wife, he said, in his bluff way, "I see how it is that the boy's craft is getting into better trim; he will not need so much watching. He was heading for the breakers when she hailed him." A few days after this, the captain said, as Zeke was leaving the house for Huldah's, "Boy, you needn't come home these short summer evenings until half past nine, unless you have a mind to!" It was the first word concerning any indulgence which Zeke had ever heard from him. His "Thank you, sir," came from a full heart.

Every evening now found Zeke at Aunt Huldah's. He was either alone in her small, homelike and always tidy kitchen, reading some books of her suggestion, or, when she was sewing, sitting near her, listening to her bewitching stories, or ever welcome words of advice. He always felt that the evenings were short. Early in their acquaintance, Huldah had asked, "Ezekiel, hast thee a copy of the Word of God?"

Zeke blushed, and said, "No ma'am." Aunt Huldah took from her small, but well-selected library, a small copy — an English edition, which was much prized by her. "Thee may'st take this for thy present use,' she remarked, placing it in his hand. "Read it daily, and pray much when thee reads. Ezekiel, dost thee pray?" Zeke answered no, by his confusion of face. "If thou prayest aright," continued Aunt Huldah, "it will bring to thee comfort in thy loneliness, and strength in thy weakness."

Zeke took the precious little volume to his room, and morning and night, read a few words of its teachings. It prepared the way for another step in the right path. It led to a constant attendance upon the Sunday services, which Aunt Huldah never neglected, though there was no society of Friends in the place. Zeke had not been often, but now he found that his going made occasion for new friendships, which brought him many kind, encouraging words. He no longer said, "I don't care," "Nobody cares for me." "I am having good luck since my acquaintance with Aunt Huldah," he said. But the utterance came from the teachings of Crone's Corner, while he heard at the same time a secret whisper in his heart, saying, "Your improved condition is God's blessing on a better life; do right and be happy."

Captain Prince was becoming tired of farming. The grounds about his house were the admiration of all persons of good taste; his fruit trees were in thrifty order, and of rare kinds; his great barn, full of hay, his granary full of many kinds of grain, and his cellars crowded with vegetables, were his pride. His live stock was large for those days, and made their owner the envy of all his neighbors, when they thought how much money they would bring, if sold. But all these things cost largely in hard work, care and cash expenditure. The owner began to fret over his farm. "It costs a mint of money, and is a great bother," he began to say. His purse felt the draft, for farming "with fancy fixings" paid no better then than now. So the captain began "to take in sail." He sold most of his stock in the fall after Zeke came, and after the fall work was done, he lived more quietly in the house, and left the chores, now easily done, to John and Zeke. Both had won his confidence, and now enjoyed its benefits, for the captain was not a man of low suspicions when he had learned to confide.

The winter came,— that winter which followed the spiritual harvest at Alden Farm and Crone's Corner,— bringing the Spirit's drawing towards Christ of Zeke, while spending his long evenings in the Christian home of Aunt Huldah. He began to feel the inspiration of that Spirit, who, all unknown to himself, was fitting him for re-union with those whom the same Holy Spirit had made new creatures in Christ.

CHAPTER XXII.

THE JUBILEE.

It was the next morning after the visit of Joel and Mary Organ to the Crones, when their confession was made, that they were talking over, with ever deepening feeling of sorrow, their agency in Zeke's long absence.

"I tell you what I am thinking," said Joel. "I am thinking that it is my duty to go, myself, and get Zeke."

"You carried him away," said his wife, sadly.

"I suppose," said Joel, smiling, "that if I go and tell Uncle Prince how mean and wicked I have been, he will nearly 'skin me.' But we are commanded to 'confess' as well as 'to forsake' our sins, and I have wronged Uncle Prince in imposing, by falsehood, Zeke upon him."

The next morning, Joel was driving over the road to the Eagle Tavern, where he had parted with Zeke. Here he took the stage, and the next evening he reached the door of Captain Prince. The uncle and nephew had always been on friendly terms, and this meeting was cordial. Joel was not long in coming to the immediate business of his visit. He stated the facts concerning Zeke, and frankly and with great tenderness and humility, rehearsed his own part in the bad transaction. The captain heard him through without interruption, but with a contracted brow and a curl of contempt upon his lips. He was not a man to appreciate the penitential tears, which, at the close of Joel's statement, stole down his face. "Joel!" he exclaimed, rising and striding across the room, "you have been contemptibly mean! Why didn't you tell me the *truth*, sir, when you sent the boy to me?" A silence followed for a moment, which appeared to Joel only the brief pause which portended a heavier explosion of the storm. "The truth, sir!" repeated the captain, in a voice of thunder, as he stopped before Joel, and fixed on him his full, fiery eye. "Why didn't you tell the *truth*, like a man!"

Another pause followed, which the captain broke by saying, in a calmer, but firm tone, "Joel Organ, leave my house at your earliest possible convenience; and never say, sir, that you are related to Captain James Prince. I will return the boy, sir, to his friends, in my own time and way."

Joel was glad, through Zeke's introduction, to breathe the forgiving atmosphere of Aunt Huldah's home, until the return of the stage, two days after the captain's denial to him of the hospitalities of his house. He was not allowed to know anything of his purposes concerning Zeke. His return home alone, with this humiliating statement of the results of his well-intended visit, was to himself and to his wife a severe test of the genuineness of their penitence; and the test proved profitable, because they bore it well.

* * * * *

The one dark spot, in the, of late, silverlined cloud, which rested upon the home at Crone's Corner, entirely disappeared when Captain James Prince entered, preceded by Zeke. The captain introduced himself with his habitual stateliness, and took the seat cordially offered. He was about to explain with dignity the reasons of his personal coming, speak a good word for Zeke, and launch his sailor's broad-side at the Organs, when he came to a stand-still, like a ship suddenly struck by a counter current, and held for the moment in the eddy. Zeke had framed most studiously, words of confession and conciliation for the ears of his offended parents. But if his return was in the spirit of the prodigal, his welcome was that of the prodigal's father. His coming had been seen, by hope and love, a great way off. Yearning hearts of tender affection were ready with the kiss and embrace of forgiveness, recognition, and welcome. The words of Ezekiel and Jerusha Crone were fewer than their tears, and both united to choke back Zeke's intended exclamation, "Father, I have sinned!" *We* have sinned, was the spirit of their salutation. "Halloo, Zeke!" shouted his sisters, Jane and Betsey, as they rushed upon him, throwing their arms around his neck and drawing him down nearly to the floor. Tom looked on and cried. He did not need to speak, or otherwise act his welcome. It was his lost brother on whom his eyes rested, and he was satisfied.

The captain looked upon the scene with surprise. Were these the parents of Zeke, who, he had for a year believed, had turned him out into the cold world! It was well

Joel was not just then present. But this feeling soon gave way to more tender emotions, and, at last, he wiped a tear from his face, the first that had moistened it since it became tanned by the sun of many climes; and, now that his heart was melted, he entered into the occasion with a generous interest. He had much to say of Zeke's great improvement the few last months, but gave the credit to his "prim neighbor," Aunt Huldah, in words as direct and forcible as those he used in reproving Joel. He closed his commendation, by saying, with a pleasant smile, which was *possible* to him, "An old sailor can *break* a colt, but it takes Aunt Huldah to make him trot round at your word, as though he loved to!"

* * * * *

When John Alden learned that Zeke had returned, and after having had repeated to him the generous words of Captain Prince, he sprang to his feet, in one of his old, generous impulses, at which Patience smiled, and in reference to which she usually had some cool, wise word of caution. "Patience!" he exclaimed, bringing his hands together with a sharp crack which startled puss from her dozing on the sunny window-seat,— "Patience! we must have a jubilee!"

"Well, John," said Patience, in a measured tone, but with a merry twinkle of her eye, "I should think your jubilee had begun!"

"Let us have," continued John, in a more subdued tone, "a day of thanksgiving. Let us kill the fatted calf. Many, that were a few months ago lost in sin, are found. The wanderer, for whom we have all mourned, has returned. Joy has come to our own home in the conversion of our boys!" The last reason given melted Mr. Alden, and he added, in a low, deep whisper, "Patience, my dear wife, we *must* have a jubilee!"

The kitchen of Alden Farm was soon jubilant with the preparations. It had often been so, but never with a more sacred joy. The pastor, the good Deacon Turner, Ezekiel Crone, the good friend William Treat, each with his entire family; Patty Vose and her mother, with a long list of the young converts, and young people — friends of Carver and Miles, were already put down among the guests. The younger members of the family discussed the coming festival, with learned wisdom. "Baby Winnie"— still the baby, though ranging the house and barn with lordly freedom — uttered his "cute" sayings, which, in the estimation of the other children, "beat all that's printed in the books."

When Ezekiel Crone learned what was going on at Alden Farm, he exclaimed, "Brother Alden is at his old business of beating us all in his good notions. But he's too fast this time! *We*, Jerusha, must have the jubilee!"

"That we must!" exclaimed his wife, with

all of her old energy, but now it was as the subduing breath of spring, compared with the freezing blast of a winter tempest. "It is *our* son who was lost and is found," she continued, "and in *our* home the feast must be made."

Alden Farm gave way to this reasonable suggestion, and the notes of preparation began to be heard at Crone's Corner. Since they had sought and found the secret of good luck in carrying out their plans, the preparations went on pleasantly. We have seen that Alden Farm itself could not excel Mrs. Crone in the manner in which she prepared her food for the table. Her husband's means had improved of late, and he provided amply for the occasion. Every room of their old house soon smiled in its perfect order and cleanliness. The children dismissed the last of the old feeling, "we are nobody," in an honest self-respect from the thought that the jubilee was at their own home, and that invitations were to go out from there, instead, as in former days, always coming to it.

Invitations were extended to all whom the Aldens proposed to invite, and were carried even further in one direction. They included some who had been known only in their opposition to those influences by which the Corner had been saved. It seemed to be Jerusha Crone's thought — for the suggestion came from her — that the songs of gladness of the saved, might be blessed to those still wandering, though they had repelled other efforts for their good.

The evening of the Jubilee at Crone's Corner came. All came quite near the hour suggested by the host. In this "olden time" the guests showed their good manners in punctuality at feasts, as well as at church, and none affected refinement by coming late. When the rooms were filled, Mr. Curtis, in behalf of the host, bid all welcome, and invited them to join in singing, "All hail the power of Jesus' name," in "Coronation." While the song was filling the house with the music of the heart, some of the loafers from the tavern looked slyly in. Their ranks had been thinned of late, by death, and still more, by desertions to the company of "Teetotalers." They had prophecied that "old Zeke's party" would be a great "fizzle," and that nobody except John Alden could make a jubilee. So they had come to see the failure. The spirit-stirring song, whose burden was the conquering name of Jesus, a glance at the crowd of happy though sober looking faces, and, to them, not least, Mrs. Crone's richly laden and tastefully arranged table, amazed them. "It beats Alden Farm folks," whispered one. "Old Zeke is awful extravagant," said another. But some lingered round, won by the pure joy of the occasion,— were invited in, and forsook from that time, the thorny path of sin.

Patty Vose was seated in a quiet corner of the parlor. "How do even children pay deference to *character*," remarked Parson Curtis, calling Deacon Turner's attention to the constant gathering of young people and little ones about the serious, but sun-shiny, and ever loving hunchback. They all consulted her in reference to their amusements, or any question of pleasant dispute which occurred.

Martha Turner, "bewitched," as the attentive eyes of certain "maiden ladies" assured them, all the "young boys." "It was ridiculous," they said, "for a deacon's daughter to act so." But it was difficult for even them to tell what wrong thing Mattie said or did. In the good sense of her remarks she was the superior of her accusers. In making the little ones happy, she excelled all others. In making the timid feel at ease, in causing the aged to confess that all respect for years on the part of the young did not leave the earth in their childhood, in scattering sunshine generally, and, especially, as a result in part of all this, making all except the meanly jealous love her, Martha Turner was a great sinner — in the estimation of the before mentioned ladies of "a certain age." Nor was it her fault that Carver Alden loved her better than he loved these ancient dames,— or even that he loved her, as it began to be whispered, better than he loved any other young person.

The Organs were present, receiving the special attention of Mr. and Mrs. Crone. Cordial forgiveness of their sin was stamped upon all countenances — except their own. Squire True's dignity was subdued by the loving freedom which breathed about him. One of the most pleasant incidents of the evening, was the entering, in the midst of the social interview, of Dr. Burt. "I have come," he said, to his old friends, "to confess my past errors, and to give to John Alden, and my pastor, and their faithful helpers, my hand of fellowship in their Christian labors, and moral reforms. I have been wrong, they have been right. My old friend, Deacon Prime, if he were living, would join me in this. The plain man of Alden Farm has conquered my prejudices, and shown, by his kind, but independent pursuit of the right, my mistake. Henceforth I am with you."

It was not late when the company broke up and sought their own homes, nor had the *feet* of any young person attempted to add anything during the gathering, to the entertainment. Brains and heart sufficed for all.

At the close of the following summer, Carver Alden entered college. His preparation was thorough for those days, for teacher and pupil agreed in careful painstaking with every lesson. He carried with him to college no unwise thought, that by "smartness," or some favoring circumstance, (by many, foolishly called "good luck,") he should secure influence and scholarship. The self-relying energy of Alden Farm, united with the cultivation of a true Christian heart, gave him a calm, steady assurance that all needed success was sure.

His brother Miles commenced his college course the next year. Less dignified, more lively than Carver, he was no less steady to principle and work.

Alden Farm, in the meantime, threw its strong protecting arm around Hope Cottage. "Patty Vose and her mother shall fail for counsel and help, only when Alden Farm fails," said Mr. Alden, and his word was a moral power.

Zeke had, with Tom, spent his leisure hours during the summer, studying and reciting to Patty Vose. They could get up early now to secure an extra hour, and not be driven to bed. The work of the farm under the united, cordial labor of father and sons, proceeded to good results.

Just before the winter came, the following letter was received at the Corner:—

"MY FRIENDS:—I have reduced my farming to a small, snug business. My man, John, leaves me this fall. Your son, Ezekiel, is just the young man for my work this winter, and I think he can take the charge of my farm next summer, for which he shall have good pay. Mrs. Prince unites with me in requesting him to come. Nancy says she 'don't want no new man fussing round;' she prefers Ezekiel. Finally, Aunt Huldah says, 'Captain, I think thee will do well to employ Ezekiel.' I know she pines for 'her boy.' So let him come.

"JAMES PRINCE."

Thus young Ezekiel Crone became the trusted foreman of the farm of Captain Prince, and was loved and counseled by the good Quaker woman, Aunt Huldah, as one taking the place of her lost son.

His brother Thomas remained at home, the intelligent, Christian young man, holding out by his steady principle and uniform industry, a good hope to his parents of comfort and support from him in old age.

So Crone's Corner rivaled Alden Farm in the "luck" which comes from a strong will and a good heart. Both families learned that

> "What most would profit us God knows,
> And ne'er denies aught good to those
> Who with their utmost strength pursue
> The right, and only care to do
> What pleases Him."

THE END.

The $1000 Prize Series.

Pronounced by the Examining Committee, Rev. Drs. Lincoln, Rankin and Day, superior to any similar series.

STRIKING FOR THE RIGHT,	$1.75
SILENT TOM,	1.75
EVENING REST,	1.50
THE OLD STONE HOUSE,	1.50
INTO THE LIGHT,	1.50
WALTER MCDONALD,	1.50
STORY OF THE BLOUNT FAMILY,	1.50
MARGARET WORTHINGTON,	1.50
THE WADSWORTH BOYS,	1.50
GRACE AVERY'S INFLUENCE,	1.50
GLIMPSES THROUGH,	1.50
RALPH'S POSSESSION,	1.50
LUCK OF ALDEN FARM,	1.50
CHRONICLES OF SUNSET MOUNTAIN,	1.50
THE MARBLE PREACHER,	1.50
GOLDEN LINES,	1.50

Sold by Booksellers generally, and sent by Mail, postpaid, on receipt of price.

BOSTON:
D. LOTHROP & CO., PUBLISHERS,
Nos. 38 & 40 CORNHILL.

www.ingramcontent.com/pod-product-compliance
Lightning Source LLC
Chambersburg PA
CBHW020104020526
44112CB00033B/918